C000071690

BEYOND THE EDGE

Jackie Greaves

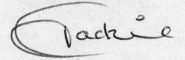

First published in Great Britain in 2010
by Caboodle Books Ltd
Copyright © Jackie Greaves

A Catalogue record for this book is available
from the British Library.

ISBN 978 0 9565 239 76

Page Layout by Highlight Type Bureau Ltd
Printed by Cox and Wyman

The paper and board used in the paperback by
Caboodle Books Ltd are natural recyclable products
made from wood grown in sustainable forests.
The manufacturing processes conform to the environmental
regulations of the country of origin.

Caboodle Books Ltd
Riversdale, 8 Rivock Avenue, Steeton, BD20 6SA
www.authorsabroad.com

With love and memory
of our lovely daughter Lesley
who was tragically killed in 1988

For some very special granddaughters

Alexandra
Charlotte
Skye
Gracie
Co Co
Honey-Mae

All the illustrations are from R. Heywood-Coyle's
delightful book 'Lakeland Penscapes'.
Further information available from
the author, 01562 882028

HELP FROM THE HILLS

There's a freshness in the mountains
Beneath the noon day sun,
Which loses not in clearness
What evening has begun.

The breezes there in summer,
A calming strength impart;
The raging winds of winter
Strike worries from the heart.

Though piercing through and bitter,
They clear away the murk,
Refreshingly to strengthen
The jaded for fresh work.

One's thoughts midst English moorlands
Drift upwards to the hills
From whence came help and gladness
With joy the spirit fills.

Majestic upland places
Where heathered hillocks roll
Those wild, wide-open spaces
Are balm within the soul.

Contents

Chapter 1

The Fight to Survive

February 1994 - I lay there lifeless, terrified and alone having fallen more than 1000 feet down Ben Macdui mountain in the Cairngorms, the second highest peak in Scotland. It was a lonely and extremely scary place to be.

The fall, through a hole in a cornice near to the summit, had been swift and unforgiving with me somersaulting like a rag doll through the air and finally landing precariously in a gully hundreds of feet above the rocks below.

Only a few short hours before, everything had been so relaxed, I had been so contented with everything going to plan. But now everything had changed. A blizzard of thick snow engulfed me and everything around me, making visibility impossible while the bitter wind stung and numbed my exposed face.

I lay there alone, having been separated only moments earlier from my two climbing companions, too terrified to move in case I plummeted further, possibly to my death. Mentally I checked myself for signs of physical injury. Although I was in pain, there seemed to be no serious damage, though psychologically I was not in a good place. I was deeply traumatised.

This wasn't meant to have happened and I was totally unprepared for it. As a seasoned climber and mountaineer, I expected things to go wrong and for weather conditions to suddenly take a turn for the worst, but this had been something else entirely Thoughts of happy times with friends and family crowded my mind together with distressing images of my grandchild, whom I feared I might never see again.

The temperature was -40°C and, although I had my full mountaineering gear on for protection including a 'Goretex' cagoule and hat, 'Buffalo' jacket and gloves, two vests, and 'Yeti' gaiters attached to my four season boots, I was still shaking uncontrollably.

Fortunately my ice axe had succeeded in halting my fall, though I had subsequently lost it in the snow during the descent, together with my crampons, which had been attached to my rucksack, and so I had no way of securing myself to the side of the mountain.

So I dug my heels in hard, my overriding instinct being to survive. There was no immediate game plan.

I wondered what measures my companions would take to raise the alarm and dared to imagine what kind of predicament they themselves might be in.

If truth be told, I had no way of predicting what would happen next. Had my companions even made it to the summit? Were they even safe and, if they were, I knew it would take hours for them to descend the mountain and get help. For the first time in my life I felt totally helpless and totally alone.

The weather continued to buffet me mercilessly and there was little way of shielding myself from its full brutish force. Instead, with freezing hands I unfastened the openings on my rucksack, which against all the odds had survived the fall intact, and inside of which was another 'Buffalo' jacket, a balaclava and gloves which I immediately put on, and then got into my survival bag. It was all I could do to sit tight and wait for a miracle to happen.

Where this would come from I had no idea as I had no sense of orientation as the white out in front of me had obliterated the sky. Never in a million years could my previous experiences of mountaineering have prepared me for this scenario, one of the worst that a climber could ever face.

I lay there too petrified to make any further movements. Thoughts raced through my mind once again, I pondered on how everything had gone so awry, so dreadfully wrong, and how this had supposed to be a half-term adventure - an escape from my responsibilities as a school secretary - to spend time doing what I loved most with like minded individuals.

Foremost in my mind was the overriding awareness that the life expectancy for someone in such a predicament was low (I was later told that, on average, this was all of twenty-five minutes in such harsh conditions). Added to this was the fact that I was only of slight build, and despite being very fit and healthy I was fifty three years of age. I also had little in the way of provisions, apart from some fruitcake, having already eaten most of the food I had with me during the ascent. I scooped up some snow and, although it hurt my tongue do so, popped it in my mouth and waited for it to melt before swallowing it for sustenance. I knew I had to try and remain conscious and that giving into the fatigue would be like sounding a death knell.

The hours seemed interminable and my mind was in turmoil. Although I had no precise way of knowing exactly what time it was, I knew it would soon be getting dark and the temperature would fall even lower. I also knew that there was no sign of rescue. There were no searchlights, no reassuring calls. There was just me and the blizzard and zero visibility. All that was keeping me going was the constant praying in my head and a strange, inexplicable light that stayed with me throughout the night. Although I knew it wasn't a searchlight it offered me comfort with its muted glow when in truth all hope seemed to be lost. Only afterwards did I question what it was. But for the present at least, it was enough just knowing that it was there.

Chapter 2

The Early Years

My childhood was a very happy one, with many wonderful memories of time spent with my loving parents and my younger brother David. As a young child I lived in Padgate not far from Warrington, Cheshire in a semi-detached house with a large garden, the type that many middle class families lived in during the forties and fifties. My father was a building agent, and as was the norm he would work regular nine to five hours, while Mum provided all the domestic securities at home. Every afternoon we would come home from school to the smell of freshly baked bread and cakes. It was an era when everything seemed so straightforward, so ordered in a way, and somehow more relaxed. In any case, life seemed a lot less hurried and frenetic than nowadays and definitely simpler. People seemed to take on traditional roles and seemed contented doing it.

As a family we were very close and at ease with one another. My mother was an open, friendly person, who had lots of confidence and because of this got involved in many things. She was a super cook and made us all good wholesome food and there was always the smell of fresh bread rising in the cooker by the fire. She liked a nice clean tidy house, cosy but without too much fussiness. She was also a wonderful gardener too and loved being outside growing vegetables and her favourite flowers such as 'lily of the valley' and 'orange blossom'. We were fortunate to have had seasonal vegetables throughout the year. Next door had a large garden, but they weren't able to use it all, so mum was able to grow more on their land and also have a greenhouse. In turn my mother would then share the vegetables with these neighbours.

My mother's own childhood had not been easy. Her mum had died when my mother was only twelve years old so Mum had had to have time off school to take charge of the house and look after her six year old brother, so life was quite tough for her in those days. Eventually my grandfather remarried and fortunately my mum got on really well with her new step-mother. Later in life my mother went to college to study for her qualifications and was able to teach cookery at a local high school. As Dad was away working in Africa it enabled her not only to earn some extra money, but to do something she loved and felt passionate about It also enabled her to make new friends.

My father in contrast was very strict with us. Everything had to be done well. He was so precise and his work was always perfect. He could turn his hand to anything though, and in our early childhood days toys weren't readily available to buy like they are nowadays, and so Dad used to make everything for us. I had a beautiful doll's house that he had made, everything perfect even down to the miniature pieces of furniture.

Despite being strict he had a kind and thoughtful nature and would do anything for us children. Both of our parents made Christmas an especially wonderful time for us children.

On Christmas Eve Dad would bring the tree home on his way back from work. It used to smell wonderfully and we used to say "Let's close our eyes and imagine we are in a pine forest on a cold snowy day." And then there would be laughter. Then Dad would fill half a beer barrel with soil and we would decorate the tree with a variety of decorations and pretty fairy lights. An assortment of decorations would be put up around the house mainly home-made paper chains and then we would sit around the fire eating our supper of buttered potato cakes.

Of course we didn't get the gifts that young ones get today - nobody did! But we were so thrilled with what we did get usually a stocking filled with an apple, a tangerine, a few boiled sweets and maybe a book and then just one main present such as a doll.

We always had a good Christmas meal together, comprising of turkey that Dad brought home on Christmas Eve plus all the trimmings following which we would play games and have tea around the fire.

As a child I always wanted to be doing things. I was restless and I never seemed to be able to just sit still and wait. I remember a couple of incidents in my life when such impatience either got me into trouble or made for highly entertaining moments. One such occasion was when Mum once left me in bed, ill with the measles, while she popped to the shops. She gave me strict instructions not to get out of bed telling me the doctor would let himself in to see me with a key she had left for him.

After she left I was bored and decided to paint using my new magic painting book but realised that I didn't have any water. So instead, I decided to use the nearest thing to hand - the potty! Needless to say the doctor duly arrived and there was I totally absorbed in my painting. He just couldn't stop laughing, remarking that he had never seen an artist work that way before. Later I got a huge telling off from my mum as she was so ashamed and embarrassed.

Another example of my exuberance as a child was when my parents left my brother and I in the house for only a short while telling us to behave ourselves and that they would be back very soon. Again the dreaded boredom set in and I was at a loss as to what to do. Then the idea came to me, "I know", I thought to myself, "I'll brand Peter the dog."

There he lay on the hearth as good as gold totally unprepared for what was about to happen. I put the poker in the fire and branded a letter 'p' in the dog's fur. He never moved a muscle and carried on lying there quite contented. There was a terrible smell of burning in the room when Mum and Dad got back and I got into real trouble when they saw what I had done. All I remember saying in my defence was that I didn't want the dog to ever get lost.

Memories like these reinforce the notion of me being restless and perhaps a little non-conformist and were certainly early indicators of the type of adventurous character I would later become. As I've got older more and more memories have bubbled to the surface in both my mind and also my brother's and quite recently he reminded me of the time that we each bored a hole in our bedroom wall with the intention of them eventually meeting in the middle so that we could talk to each other at night time. It took us weeks to get through and when we did we covered the hole with a flap of wallpaper. When our father found out, he was so cross and we ended up being grounded for weeks.

But despite these usual childish high jinks, as I would call them, and the ensuing trouble this always got me into, I was a relaxed and contented child and I enjoyed outdoor life to the full, particularly climbing trees and building dens, which we seemed to do with total abandon from morning till night during the weekends and summer holidays. Every year we helped with the haymaking and the potato picking on the local farm close to our home.

I've already mentioned that as a family we also used to grow vegetables in the back garden and I used to love going out and digging up potatoes for tea the same evening, a practise I have continued to do to this day. Our garden was large and we had chickens at the bottom of it and I loved going out and collecting the eggs. which were usually still warm and so fresh to eat.

The 'milk and veg' man used to come round on a horse and cart and I remember quite vividly that it was my job to collect the horse manure quickly before anyone else got it as it was so good for our vegetables. So I was handed a shovel and bucket and got on with my job of collecting the manure, which was still warm. What a task!

Other memories that still make me smile include hitching a lift to school on the back of the 'pea wagon' and eating the shelled peas en route. I can remember the experience as if it were yesterday - the delicate scent of the vegetables and each bumpy turn in the road. That, and getting a lift on the 'milk wagon' and sitting there amongst the jangling bottles of milk.

When I got home from school I would be greeted by our loveable blue budgie, Micky, who would give us so many laughs. He would chase Peter the dog scaring him to death, pecking at his nose while he was having a quiet moment by the fire. Micky also used to recite nursery rhymes such as 'Georgy Porgy' and when Mum walked through the room he would shout "Hurry up, Mum". He was lovely and so entertaining!

From our annual holidays spent with friends on the Island of Alderney in the Channel Islands to the time spent playing netball and taking part in running events at school, it was a carefree period in my life, which I now look back on with great affection.

Being on Alderney each year in particular was great fun especially as we stayed on a farm. This meant we were able to ride on the tractors around the fields, help make the haystacks, collect eggs and feed the chickens. There were also lots of sea cliff walks and lovely beaches where we could go off and wander and explore for the day.

Dad would drive to the port and we would sail to Alderney, which of course was all part of the excitement of the holiday.

One year, because Dad was in the Royal Engineers on Alderney, and was in charge of getting the airstrip up and running again, we flew in a small plane. As you can imagine it was so exciting as we had never experienced anything like it before

Some years we would go to South Wales to stay in an Aunt's cottage, where we would be up early collecting raspberries, blackcurrants and eggs and then Auntie would make gorgeous pies for tea. A couple of times we went to the Lake District, which was a long drive in those days with no M6 motorway to make life easier.

I have extremely fond memories of my schooldays but I do remember on the first day deciding not to stay there, so I followed my mum back home. She was very cross and marched me back pronto. Once I'd settled in I really enjoyed it, and used to sing in the choir and on stage. I don't know how that came about as I have an awful singing voice!

I would say I was quite academic but I didn't put it into practise as I was far more interested in sport. I was captain of the netball team, represented the school at hockey and also ran regularly for the school. That said, I was far from being a model pupil- I used to get into trouble. Mostly this was as a result of talking too much but I remember once doing something exceptionally naughty. I put some fake dog dirt on the floor near the cookery teacher's desk. Understandably she was very cross, as she thought it was real and that someone had let a dog into the room until she realised what it was. I got into serious trouble for that one.

From time to time I also used to get into bother for scrumping. Being chased by the farmer and caught up a tree seemed to be the norm for me. I used to hide the apples in my jacket hood and once put them inside my knicker leg thinking the farmer wouldn't notice that I was walking funny. For me though, it all represented innocent childish fun.

I loved being a member of the St John's Ambulance Brigade from the age of about eight to twelve. We would meet up once a week in a hut near Padgate Station, where we would practise first aid work including learning to bandage injuries and how to give assistance to an injured person until the medic came. I thoroughly enjoyed it and remember being very interested in helping those in need. We were often on duty at rugby matches and at the cinemas in Warrington, which came with the added bonus that we could also watch whatever was being shown at that time. In conjunction with this, there were the parades which we often took part in alongside the 'Walking Day' processions.

Life up until I was about nine had continued in this pattern, contented, steadfast but largely uneventful But all that was about to change when my father responded to an advert for the post of

'Building Agent' in Kumasi, on the Gold Coast of West Africa, which is now known as Ghana, overseeing the building of a local hospital and subsequently he succeeded in getting the job. At the time, in my child's mind, I couldn't fully comprehend what this meant, although after he had left I found the enforced absence and the loneliness of him not being there, naturally upsetting. Together with the sporadic communication available to us, this led me to miss him terribly.

For about twelve years, my mother had to bring us up alone, which must have been an enormous strain and extremely tiring and difficult at times. Not that we saw this though as children. There would have been all the chores to do without the assistance of modern conveniences such as washing machines and vacuum cleaners, the management of all the finances and bills, the maintenance of the house as well as feeding and looking after us two. She never seemed overwhelmed or flustered though and must have been a pretty resilient character really. We never felt short of love or affection or really short of anything.

The close neighbourhood that we lived in then must have been a comfort to her and people looked out for each other in those days It was very much close knit, as it was the norm for mums to stay at home with children in those days. There would also have been the relatives she had in the area but still it would have been tough. As we got older she didn't really tell us about this time. Parents in my generation weren't as open with their feelings even when their children became adults, not like today where there is far less formality between the generations and things are more openly discussed. I like to think that today's older generation are seen to be far more in touch with their emotions and in turn more modern than previous more remote generations, though I don't feel I was any worse off for this. We were contented and that was all that mattered. I must admit though, that it is only now, looking back after having raised a family of my own and being a grandmother of six, that I recognise how difficult a period this must have been in my mother's life to have taken on sole responsibility for everything and for such a long duration.

Chapter 3

Africa

After an absence of about three years, my parents made the decision for us to follow my father to Africa. It was a very brave step for my mother to take, especially as she would be travelling half way across the world as a lone parent with two children to a backwater, as it was then, that she had never even set eyes on before. It was also treacherous for other reasons, namely rabies that was prevalent there, though we had been vaccinated at Liverpool Tropical Disease Centre against smallpox, typhoid, yellow fever and tetanus. There would also be deadly spiders and venomous snakes, which we would have to contend with, making life far more precarious. Added to this we would be taken away from all we knew, from the familiarity of our home and loved ones, our daily routines and formal education to an alien world, where we would be home schooled and also where we would have house helpers.

In a matter of weeks everything would be different, from the food and the climate to the culture and the environment. Looking back my mother showed great resolve and strength in making that decision and following it through. This was made even harder as she would be leaving behind her support network of family and friends. To us children it seemed like one big adventure and more importantly for us it signified a longed for reunion with our father.

We set sail from Liverpool docks on a dismal January morning in

17

1954 with friends and relatives waving us off from the embankment. I can see the ship now, the *Aureol*, it was a huge 14,000 tonne ocean liner, belonging to the 'Elder Demster' Lines, which would be our home for the fifteen days it would take to get us to Africa. We were so excited to be embarking on this voyage and everything seemed like one big adventure.

Life on the ship was really great for us children with lots of entertainment provided, including sports –swimming, tennis, deck quoits together with a cinema and regular parties. I even managed to win the greasy pole fight over the pool, which proved to be a talking point for days afterwards. The living conditions were very comfortable, with pleasant cabins and varied and wholesome meals. On the whole it was a relaxed time and not at all stressful or worrisome, well not for the children at least. Going through the Bay of Biscay however was a different matter. The sea was so rough that the boat rolled about precariously causing everybody to be extremely seasick. All the crockery on board was smashed and we were later informed that it had been the worst crossing ever. Gradually though, the choppiness subsided and we soon came into calmer waters and hotter climates as we approached the coast of Africa.

Being able to stop off at different ports en route was a real education for us. In particular I remember the beautiful volcanic island of the Gran Canaria together with Freetown and Sierra Leone. Finally we arrived at Takoradi in West Africa, a very busy port with locals running around and shouting excitedly in their native Housa tongue as our liner approached.

My first memory was of the effervescent locals, together with the heat and pungent air, and then of our luggage being hauled off the boat in a great big net before we finally greeted our father with big bear hugs and embraces. He didn't seem to have changed much, especially in his demeanour. He was the same Dad we had always known, warm-hearted and affectionate.

We would be living in a place called Kumasi some 200 miles from the port and we were directed towards Dad's Jeep, which would take us to the place we would call home for the next two years. The scenes of everyday life as we travelled were a real eye opener; locals on 'mammy wagons, a type of bus - while others ran alongside them in order to clamber aboard. The vistas and backdrop were as far removed from life back home as you could imagine, with lush vegetation as far as the eye could see and huge banana trees dominating the landscape. The heat was constant causing flies to stick to our faces incessantly and the air was dusty from the African road in front.

When we arrived at our destination it looked like a little clearing on the fringe of the African bush. Our home was a single, two storey, white pebble-dashed dwelling with a veranda on the front and netted windows. Inside the living areas were Spartan - but comfortable enough with bedrooms for all and other amenities such as electric lighting - always unpredictable - together with an unreliable, though flushing loo.

There to greet us when we arrived were two 'houseboys' called Mama and Hillary whose responsibility it was to undertake some of the domestic duties. That night we settled down to a basic meal of local produce - avocadoes, pineapple and sweet potato and later slept in beds not altogether dissimilar to the ones we had left back home but more basic.

From then onwards our morning routine would comprise of washing at an inside sink, a breakfast of cornflakes bought from a supermarket in the nearest town fifteen miles away, followed by home tutoring by my father's friend, a university lecturer, for one hour, then some relaxation and playtime.

There were few other English people that we came into contact with apart from when we visited our local town and bought provisions and an occasional chocolate treat, together with our weekly visit to the Konongo gold mines, to meet up with other Brits, usually army families. In reality we didn't really mind as we had each other and made friends with the locals, who we became very fond of.

Hillary in particular, a cheerful looking thick set lad in his thirties, always proved to be a constant source of entertainment. I remember one time in particular when my father bought him a bike, the likes of which he had never seen before let alone actually ridden. Needless to say, unused to pedalling, he kept falling off but then would be laughing so much that he wouldn't be able to get back on again.

Very often we would hear the sound of tom toms and chanting from outlying villages and soon became familiar with the frequent severe storms that would blow up from nowhere, and which would cut off the electricity supply from our generator in the garden. This would lead to us battening down the hatches to ride out the bad weather. Hillary used to rush round lighting the oil lamps and more often than not no sooner had he lit them than Dad would have got the generator working again, which caused so much laughter time after time.

That was not the only thing we had to contend with. Cockroaches were permanently in the house, together with the occasional scorpion, and each night we had mosquito nets over our beds and had to check under our covers for unwanted guests. Tarantula spiders roamed outside while lizards resided on the house walls. The ants in West Africa were huge and their ant hills five feet high on occasion. Very often when we were collecting pawpaws (a cross between a melon and a peach, which were delicious), my brother, Hillary and I would get covered in the insects and would have to roll over and over in the grass to try to get rid of them.

Because of the tropical climate, all native fruits were huge, including oranges and lemons, and so tasty. Avocados were plentiful around our house and we often ate them and coconuts with our meals.

All our cooking was done by Mama, our houseboy, but he was hopeless. Mum had to teach him a few things. We once brought in some bananas from the garden and asked him to make some custard to accompany them. Shortly after we heard a lot of clattering coming from the kitchen area. When we asked if everything was alright, he replied "I'm just making some fried custard, Mam". Needless to say, it was awful and we fell about laughing.

As a teenager, experiences like these made Africa a vibrant and exciting place for me, and life was very much for living. Not long after we arrived we acquired a chimpanzee called Ja Ja, I seem to recall a friend of my father's bringing him round one day and us adopting him. He was adorable and would sit at the table eating cornflakes with us, then put the bowl on his head and clap his hands as a sign that he wanted more. He was wonderful company and went everywhere with us, holding our hands like a small child. Being part of the family we used to dress him in pants with small braces which he loved, and later we got him a small bike which he would ride round on, ringing its bell.

Without doubt it was a magical time for us children, and we felt privileged to be there. But saying that, there were also many terrifying moments. I loved to swim and had no fear of the water but that hadn't always been the case for my brother. I remember a time when we were on holiday, before we went to Africa, and were staying at Porthmadoc in North Wales. I was about six and my brother four when he decided to paddle in the sea. Suddenly from nowhere a motorboat appeared, leaving quite a strong wake in its tracks, into which my brother was sucked. Within seconds the current had dragged him out into deeper waters. Without even thinking, and ignoring my mother's pleas not to go any further, I went in after my brother and pulled him from the water. Probably that hair-raising incident had instilled in my mother the need for my brother to learn to swim and, by the time we arrived in Africa, both he and I were strong swimmers.

We used to love wading into the man made pool at the Konongo gold mines - a clean stretch of water with vegetation surrounding it on all sides. The water would be cool and fresh and very inviting and on average we used to take a dip there every week.

One particular day I remember frolicking in the water when a black mamba snake suddenly coiled itself around my leg. I knew instantly that I was in trouble and screamed for help. Fortunately an African friend came to my aid and chopped its head off with his bare hands. What I didn't know at the time was that the black mamba is a deadly snake, and that the venom of its bite kills within twenty minutes. All of the African people seemed so strong and had no fear. They always killed any snakes that were roaming around and there were many deadly ones which used to roam around freely through the vegetation in and around our garden. This was to be the first of many lucky escapes.

On another occasion I had had agonising stomach pains for about two weeks and nobody including the hospital doctors knew what was wrong. As a last resort, one of our houseboys brought in a witch doctor from one of the villages in the jungle outside of the shanty territory we lived in. He was dressed all in orange and his face was painted in a similar colour interspersed with white. He began to dance around me, chanting words as he did so. After this had continued for about fifteen minutes, he proceeded to smear Vaseline, which my mother had provided, onto my belly button. Almost instantaneously, to my relief and everybody else's utter horror, a worm came wriggling out. This was such a physical relief as almost immediately the pain stopped.

Apparently a Tumbu fly had laid some eggs and one had somehow become attached to me. When it hatched the worm had burrowed its way into my flesh, where it had been gorging itself and residing ever since. How revolting! The Vaseline had cut off its oxygen supply causing it to feel suffocated and to search for air, hence its timely appearance. Needless to say it was not an occurrence for the faint hearted!

I have since read about another lady who had had a similar bite while holidaying in Kenya. This lady, who was only in her twenties and from England, had had all the requisite jabs, had spent a small fortune on ant-malarial pills, and was almost constantly doused in mosquito repellent. She even wore an old T shirt while snorkelling to make sure her back didn't get burned and to avoid any bites.

However on the way home in the taxi she noticed that she had what she thought was a single mosquito bite. It was on the inside of her left upper arm, by the seam of her T shirt, but she wasn't too bothered as it wasn't even itchy and she thought that the cool air-conditioning of the plane might dry it out. But the reality was somewhat different.

Within a few hours of arriving home she was being violently sick but didn't associate this with the bite, assuming that it was food poisoning or a bug from the plane. After twenty four sleepless hours she noticed that the bite was getting bigger and it was now the size of a grain of rice. It was infected as it had become yellow and hard. Two days later she was no longer ill but the bite was so painful that she was exhausted by it as the pain was so relentless. It was now very raised and very yellow and she was both repulsed and pained by it.

On her third night back home the pain was so intense that she was again unable to sleep. It was a sharp pain as if someone had put a knitting needle in the freezer and was jabbing it into her arm. By now there was a hole at the top of the bite and pus was oozing out of it. Not only that, but also, quite horrifically, it seemed to be moving. She went to the Royal Free Hospital in London, where a doctor from the tropical disease unit saw her and she was diagnosed as having been bitten by a Tumbu fly. Like me, the larva of the Tumbu fly had burrowed under her skin.

Apparently the Tumbu fly can be found anywhere in the tropics from South America and India through to Australasia and Thailand. Both myself and the lady described above had the condition known as myiasis, where larvae live and feed on a host. It sounds disgusting but is relatively rare in humans. Apparently the female Tumbu fly likes to lay its eggs on damp clothing or linen. If those clothes are then worn, the eggs penetrate the skin. After two or three days the larvae hatch beneath the skin. Once born the larvae need air so they eat their way out hence the pain. Some of the worms head in the right direction to the surface others burrow further inwards, which makes the process of removal much more difficult.

I later found out that in the Tropics it is important not to wear damp clothes that have been outside. Clothes should be tumble dried or, if they are left to dry outside, ironed as the intense heat kills the eggs. The same is true for swimming costumes. Never leave them hanging on your hotel balcony to dry in the sun while you take a nap. The lady's treatment was very similar to my own using Vaseline slathered over the area and an airtight plastic dressing placed on top. So I haven't been the only one to encounter the dreaded Tumbu!

This wasn't the only nasty episode I had during my time out there Things took another ugly turn for the worse shortly after this. When I was out walking alone one day a local dog, totally unprovoked, suddenly bit me on the arm, drawing a little blood. Naturally I screamed with shock but was completely panic-stricken when I turned and saw that the dog was frothing at the mouth and had started to fit. This meant only one thing - Rabies! To add to the whole trauma, not long after biting me, the dog just dropped down dead in front of me.

I was distraught, fearing imminent death and was urgently transported to the local hospital where I was given a very painful injection in my bottom using a large needle. This was repeated every day for the next twenty seven days. Despite feeling no adverse symptoms from the bite I knew that the injections were vital to my recovery and, although I dreaded the treatment, without them I would certainly not have lived to tell the tale. Following the incident I was under observation from the doctors for several weeks but fortunately didn't suffer any ill health. It is still a cause of much hilarity in my family, that the dog after having bit me should die and I should live. I felt that it was typical that these things should happen to me but despite their traumatic nature it always seemed that someone somewhere was looking out for me and keeping me safe.

I later found out that rabies or hydrophobia is a viral neuroinvasive disease that causes acute encephalitis (inflammation of the brain) in warm-blooded animals. The term is derived from the Latin for 'madness', which in turn may have come from the Sanskrit rabhas 'to do violence'. It is zoonotic i.e. it is transmitted by animals, most commonly by a bite from an infected animal but occasionally by other forms of contact. Generally fatal if left untreated, it is a significant killer of livestock in some countries.

From the point of entry, the virus travels quickly along the neural pathways into the central nervous system and then into other organs including the brain. The incubation period of the disease depends on how far the virus must travel to reach the central nervous system, usually taking a few months. The salivary glands receive high concentrations of the virus thus allowing further transmission. During this phase the virus cannot be easily detected within the host. However, once the infection reaches the central nervous system and symptoms begin to show, the untreated infection is usually fatal within days.

The period between infection and the first flu-like symptoms is normally two to twelve weeks, but can be as long as two years. Early-stage symptoms of rabies are malaise, headache and fever, later progressing to more serious ones, including acute pain, violent movements, uncontrolled excitement, depression, confusion and inability to swallow water (hence the name hydrophobia). Finally the patient may experience periods of mania, terror, paranoia and hallucinations, inability to quench his or her thirst and terror when presented with liquids followed by coma. The primary cause of death is usually respiratory failure.

Apparently most animals can be infected by the virus and can transmit the disease to humans. Infected bats, monkeys, raccoons, foxes, skunks, cattle, wolves, coyotes, dogs, mongoose (normally yellow mongoose) and cats provide the greatest risk to humans. Rabies may also spread through exposure to infected domestic farm animals, groundhogs, weasels, bears and other wild carnivores. Rodents (mice, squirrels etc) are seldom infected.

Three stages of rabies are recognised in dogs and other animals. The first stage is a one to three day period characterised by behavioural changes and is known as the 'prodromal' stage. The second stage is the 'excitable' stage, which lasts three to four days. It is this stage that is often known as furious rabies due to the tendency of the affected animal to be hyper-reactive to external stimuli and bite at anything near. The third stage is the 'paralytic' stage and is caused by damage to motor neurons. Lack of coordination is seen due to rear limb paralysis and drooling and difficulty swallowing caused by paralysis of face and of throat muscles

The virus is usually present in the nerves and saliva of a rabid animal and therefore the route of infection is usually, but not necessarily, by a bite. In many cases the infected animal is exceptionally aggressive, may attack without provocation, and exhibit otherwise uncharacteristic behaviour. Transmission between humans is extremely rare, though a few cases have been recorded through transplant surgery.

Shockingly there are an estimated 55,000 human deaths annually worldwide from rabies, with about 31,000 in Asia and 24,000 in Africa. One of the reasons for the recent growth of rabies in East Asia is the pet boom. Because of this China introduced to the city of Beijing the 'one dog policy' in November, 2006 to control the problem. India has been reported as having the highest rate of human rabies in the world, primarily because of stray dogs.

Rabies was once rare in the United States outside the Southern states but nowadays, skunks are the primary carriers of rabies in the midwestern states, comprising 134 of the 237 documented non-human cases in 1996. However, in the US since the widespread vaccination of domestic dogs and cats and the development of effective human vaccines, the number of recorded deaths from rabies has dropped from one hundred or more annually in the early twentieth century to one or two per year mostly caused by bat bites, which may go unnoticed by the victim and hence untreated.

From my own research on this topic, I have subsequently found out that there are only six known cases of a person having survived symptomatic rabies and only two known cases of survival in which the patient received no rabies-specific treatment either before or after illness onset. Unfortunately most of these survivors were left with severe brain damage. Indeed almost every infected case with rabies resulted in death until a vaccine was developed by Louis Pasteur and Emile Roux in 1885. Treatment after exposure, known as post-exposure prophylaxis (PEP) is highly successful in preventing the disease if administered promptly, generally within ten days of infection. In cases where there has been a significant delay in administering PEP, the treatment should be administered regardless of the delay, as it may still be effective if it is not too late.

Despite these incidents Lady Luck always seemed to be on my side, and this was particularly evident on one occasion, when my father, brother and I were out driving one day in Dad's Land Rover through the jungle. A terrific storm blew up from nowhere, causing lightning to strike surrounding trees and to fall and obstruct our path. We found ourselves immobilised and stuck in that jeep for hours with darkness approaching.

Added to this sense of isolation and fear, was the fact that we were in the middle of nowhere, with just jungle vegetation surrounding us. I distinctly remember a scorpion sitting precariously close to us on the dash board, and a couple of poisonous snakes crawling in and around our jeep. With no other option available to us, we tried to shift the trees but to no avail. Then to our mounting panic and disbelief, we heard the sound of tom toms in the distance getting progressively louder. After a short while, which seemed to us like an eternity, a full African tribe appeared, men, women, children, all dressed up in native attire with painted faces, who then proceeded to dance around us. They began chanting loudly, thrusting their spears in the air, and there we were, in the middle, totally terrified.

It soon became clear that they wanted our money and valuables. After a lot of arguing, Dad decided to give in and give them his watch. Luckily, this seemed to placate them, and having accepted it they decided to help us move the trees. Without their help I cannot imagine what might have happened to us, as we were in the middle of the jungle, with no provisions, no way of signalling for help and at the mercy of the jungle inhabitants.

When Dad's contract came to an end and he informed us that the time had come to return home. We were naturally upset but also excited at the same time. We were sorry to be leaving Hillary and Mama and knew we would miss our lives in Kumasi dreadfully as we had been so happy there. Africa had definitely left its mark on us but we knew in our hearts that it was time to go.

Chapter 4

Home Again

Coming back from Africa was quite a shock. We had loved it there and had fitted in very easily with the people and the place. It had been such a laid-back life both in terms of the culture and the locals. Back in England everything seemed so noisy and full of hustle and bustle. What had seemed so normal to us before we left England now seemed so alien, and everything was different again. However, children in particular are pretty resilient, and we soon settled into our old lives again, re-establishing friendships and resuming school – in my case for my final year. All I remember is picking up where I left off really.

Because I had had private tuition in Africa I wasn't aware of having fallen behind in any way, and I just seemed to adapt to my circumstances once again. Not much fuss was made about where we had been by those around us and I think because of this we didn't really view it as being anything really extraordinary. I had my family with me here as I had done there, and as such, I don't really remember pining for what I had left behind.

I think the adventurous spirit that later led me to climb, could be seen in me then as, I think inside I was quite resilient despite being on the shy side socially and not too perturbed by my change of circumstances. To be honest I've never been one to be fazed by change, I like to think I embrace it. As for becoming attached to things, well they're just material aren't they. I've always had a great attachment to family and close friends though and did miss Mama and Hillary when we left Africa as they had become part of the family. But the decision had been made to return home and we just had to accept that.

On finishing at Culcheth High School, I was sent to a private school to undertake English studies which included shorthand and typing. I enjoyed it but it was hard work. We had to write out the front page of the daily newspaper in shorthand every night and then translate it back to our tutor in the morning. That combined with the other homework we had to do, made it hard graft and we got into quite a lot of trouble if the work wasn't done, and done promptly. It was probably the intensity of study and the discipline needed that was one of the biggest eye-openers after having been in Africa as everything there was so laid-back and care-free. Here I had to knuckle done if I wanted to get my qualifications and get a good job; but it was all good preparation for the school secretary jobs that I would later hold and the organisational and administrative skills needed.

I remember my teenage years in a very positive way very active and full I was still very heavily into my sport - netball, hockey running and cycling. I also had quite an engaging social life too and would frequently travel with my friends by train from Warrington to Liverpool to sail on the ferryboats, where traditional jazz was played on board. Saturday evenings were brilliant and very much anticipated. Acker Bilk used to play in the clubs there together with other well-known jazz players. The infamous Cavern Club, where the Beatles used to play, was another favourite haunt of ours. The buzz in the place was electric - everybody crowded into this relatively small, smoky, dim-lit place, full of excitement and anticipation and enjoying the heady atmosphere. Of course at the time we didn't know that history was in the making and that many of the groups that were around at that time would define the era so strongly and add to the whole musical culture of the north, and in fact the whole world. To think that we were a part of that scene still amazes me and makes me feel extremely privileged to this day.

Despite the prevalence of rock and roll and the headiness of it all, for my friends and I, it was still quite a chaste and innocent time in many ways. I had to be home by a set time each evening, and was only allowed to drink Pepsi Cola while I was out. Alcohol simply wasn't available. Nobody was staggering around drunk, especially not the girls, and we felt safe being out at that time. Even though we were in the city centre crime just wasn't like it is now.

Other favourite places of ours were the Iron Door club and the Mardi Gras, where again the ubiquitous rock and roll music was played. It was great for dancing, relaxing and just being yourself, and I often went there with friends. When I was eighteen I met Roy, my future husband, at a friend's party. He was eighteen months older than me, with longish blonde hair, a slim build and fine features. Like me he loved the outdoors and also enjoyed football and motorcycling. He put me at ease straight away as he was such an easy-going character. The evening that we met he took me home on the back of his motorbike, which didn't go down at all well with my parents, as they knew nothing about him and they were strict. That said, after he popped round the following night to pick up the gloves he had left behind and Mum and Dad had invited him in, they soon realised what a decent and likeable chap he was. From then on he was just like one of the family. My dad and Roy had a lot to talk about as they were both in the building trade and my mum would get a nice steak in for him if he was coming round, which became a regular occurrence.

Like me Roy came from a happy background but it was slightly different to my own. For a start his parents owned pubs, which meant he could play in large open spaces on the premises, such as the bowling green. Despite not being happy as a boarder at the age of eleven at a private school called Rossall in Blackpool, he later went to board at a school in Shropshire called Cloverley Hall, where he was much more contented. He had a younger sister Marion, and Roy and I were very lucky as Marion and my brother David both got on well with their siblings' partners.

Roy's bike gave us a lot of freedom to go out and enjoy ourselves and we would regularly go ice-skating at Altrincham Ice Rink in the evenings and dancing at Frodsham. Flared skirts and starched underskirts were very much the fashion then and we used to stiffen the underskirts in the bath with sugar before going to the Dance Halls. I thought I looked the bees-knees as we all did at the time. I never stopped to think what I must have looked like riding pillion on a motorbike dressed like that and with a motorcycle helmet on too! I must have been blinded by love or something. Whatever it was Roy must have been blinded by it too!

After a courtship of four years, Roy and I got married in 1964 at Christ Church, Padgate. It was quite a large affair and we had a lovely reception at the Cottage Hotel in Thelwall. Following that we honeymooned in Jersey in the Channel Islands and began our married life in Bircham Newton, Norfolk, where Roy was now stationed with the RAF. We stayed there for a few years and although it was a charming and pretty place it was very much out in the sticks. There was very little traffic, no shops, no telephone, and once a week vans would come with groceries, fish and other provisions, which was how we would do our shopping. A small Mobile Library would come round with a steady stream of books.

Because of this sense of isolation, life could be lonely and days could go by without me seeing anyone. We had our first child, David, there in 1965 and stayed for the next few years. Despite the remoteness of Bircham Newton, Sandringham wasn't very far away and there were lovely beaches, which we could visit. I distinctly remember visiting the place and admiring the lavender fields all around us filling the air with their beautiful scent.

When Roy left the RAF in 1967 we moved from Norfolk and bought our home in Lowton, where our first daughter, Sharon, was born in the same year. Then in 1969 our third child, Lesley, was born. We stayed in that home for thirty-seven years and were extremely happy there bringing up our children. I didn't work at that time. My priority was my family. I was always there for the children when they came in from school, ready with the homemade cakes, much as my own mother had done. Family life was a great joy to me, and it was with this in mind that we bought a small tent which we would tow on a trailer into Wales. Later we would advance to a larger one.

The children loved those holidays, being able to run around and explore. One memory in particular is etched in my mind. We pitched in a place we thought was perfect but soon found out in the early hours of the morning that it was directly behind a cowshed, accompanied by corresponding sound and smells! Needless to say the children thought it was hilarious.

We also had lots of happy holidays in the Lake District where we stayed in a converted barn at Hawkshead. We spent enjoyable times walking and exploring the countryside, making dens in trees and orienteering. The children loved this especially when darkness was approaching and they used to scramble and play in waterfalls, making dams across the streams.

Later, again in pursuit of the outdoor life, we decided to buy a large caravan on Anglesey, where we took our holidays for many years. On Fridays we would leave straight after school and come back late Sunday night. We did lots of walking and fishing and there was a lovely private beach, where it was quite safe for our children to play. I remember one time when David caught a sea bass, He was so delighted and pleased with himself to have outwitted it.

We also spent some happy holidays in Guernsey, in the Channel Islands; the freedom and abandon, which the children just loved. While there David could indulge in his love of fishing. Once much to his delight, there was a huge tug on the line and when he reeled in the heavy weight on the end, he was amazed to see that it was a conger eel. It caused such a flurry of excitement. But we did the right thing and shortly after we threw it back into the sea.

Another time he caught whiting, which we took back to our hotel, where the chef kindly cooked them for David's meal. The fact that he had actually caught them himself made the experience unforgettable. After many years, when the children were older, we decided to sell the caravan and started motoring to France, where we would stay in caravans on site. To be perfectly honest it didn't really matter to the kids where we were as long as they had the freedom to roam and explore within a safe setting.

Thinking about my own children's childhood, it's the funny little episodes, that didn't seem so funny at the time that stand out. I often smile when people mention their children's pets as we had them all. I remember when the children were young, Roy made a model railway in our loft, all set out with hills, bridges, tunnels and stations. It was really great. One night while we were in bed we heard a lot of noise. It transpired that David, our son, had taken his pet mice up to the loft while playing with the trains and they had escaped. Needless to say they had multiplied and this particular night were having a great time scampering around the model station and nibbling at the scenery. As you can imagine we had a real job on our hands finding them all but we eventually succeeded.

We also had rabbits, and one time after coming back from our caravan at about midnight, extremely tired, the children persuaded us to allow them to nip outside to say goodnight to them. When they got there they had a lovely surprise; there were babies, so we spent the next couple of hours warming them in the lounge our tiredness quickly having left us. Added to this we also had a ferret, which gave Roy a nasty bite whilst showing the children how to feed it properly, together with gerbils, which used to keep us awake whizzing around their wheel. Later we had a dog. It was quite a menagerie!

Another funny incident involving the children was when David went camping with the Scouts. All the children were in the Scouts and Guides. On this occasion he had been chosen to cook for his team, and accordingly I gave him all the ingredients he needed but advised him to keep the salad cool by keeping it in water as the weather was so hot. We all went to visit him the next day and he turned to me and said 'I've done what you said, Mum, I've put the salad in the water to keep it cool'. So I looked around for a bowl or a bucket full of salad, but there was nothing. It turned out that instead he had put it all in the nearby stream, the lettuce, tomatoes, the lot!

There they were all merrily floating downstream with the current. I ended up wading in to rescue them and trying to save what was left for tea. But I couldn't be angry with him as he had only done as he was asked, just a little too literally!

On leaving school, the children wanted to go off on holiday on their own. All of them had attended Leigh College in Lancashire, where they sat their GCSEs with David going on to become an Underwriter and Sharon going to Royal Holloway University in London, studying French and English, and later becoming a journalist.

When Sharon gained her Degree the awards ceremony was held in the Royal Albert Hall and Princess Anne presented her with her qualification. We were so proud and it was wonderful to experience such a lovely service in such a beautiful setting. Lesley, our youngest, went straight into a job on leaving school at the UK Atomic Energy Authority in Risley, Warrington.

She spent most of her teenage years looking after and riding her horse, Lucky. Between them they won lots of medals and rosettes. She loved her horse and spent all her time at the stables and we all used to enjoy watching her compete in the shows. All of our three children took part in the Duke of Edinburgh Award scheme. David and Lesley got their 'silver' and Sharon gained a gold award and did her 'silver' in Switzerland. To receive the award we were invited to St Jame's Palace, London. It was a lovely service and the Duke of Edinburgh himself presented the awards. Sharon then went on to work with the Duke of Edinburgh Award scheme in Iceland, living in tents for about six weeks. She absolutely loved it.

It was great to see my children settled and forging out careers in their chosen fields. As is the norm with children, they all had their own distinct personalities and interests but they were all very family orientated, loving and easy-going children who gave us untold joy and very little cause for concern as they were growing up.

Chapter 5

The Call of the Mountains.

Climbing and fellwalking had become an increasingly strong passion of mine, and with the freeing up of more time, Roy and I were able to go more and more often. In particular I used to travel to Scotland for long weekends and walk the ridges there, sometimes only coming down in the evenings in the darkness. Roy, in the early years enjoyed going on his motorbike, Honda Pan European, on tours around Europe. In later years he sold the motorbike to do more walking with me particularly around the Lakeland ridges.

Island on Grasmere

When I was younger, I also used to go ice-climbing, which really got the adrenalin pumping. This combination of fear and excitement really made me feel alive and I remember one occasion in particular when we had to wade through icy waters with our boots tied round our necks.

Given the chance, we would climb up the high snowy mountains and sleep in our sleeping bags watching the dawn break. Other times we used to stay in Bunkhouses and converted barns.

Looking back I must have been incredibly fit. Most Wednesday evenings during this time were taken up with cycling to Anglezarke at Rivington with all my climbing gear hanging from the handlebars and over my shoulders and my climbing helmet tied to the back of the seat. We had great fun climbing different routes and the friendships made were an added bonus. We used to have a long cycle home tired but happy. For me, each evening of the rest of the week was taken up by a thirty mile cycle ride, whatever the weather.

The Aonach Eagach at Glen Coe, is one of the finest if not the best ridge walks in Scotland and major winter mountaineering expeditions are regularly undertaken there together with exhilarating scrambling. For us, climbing there was a much awaited adventure. We travelled there one icy February day during the half term break and experienced what seemed like all four seasons in one day, ice, sun, snow and mist, and we had to tread extremely carefully as the conditions were so icy and slippery.

The rope was needed on several occasions as parts of the ascent were near to graded rocks. It took many exhilarating hours to climb and looking down from on high on the exposed vista emphasised the need for a really good head for heights on the part of the climber. Once on the ridge, there is no way off except by pushing forwards. Added to this is that part of it comprises very polished rock, signifying that the only way to descend is to face the rock and be very sure footed. The views at the top, needless to say, were spectacular, and when we returned to the Clachaig Inn in Glen Coe we were high on adrenalin and extremely contented. A few pints of Guinness and a meal by the fire rounded off the day nicely.

The Cobbler in the Arrochar Alps in Southern Scotland was another firm favourite of mine. I have climbed this many times, always in winter conditions, necessitating great care and attention as the summit is very exposed. As a result it is a very exhilarating scramble especially as we had to crawl through an exposed window and along airy ledges. Four of us slept all night on top of this mountain in thick snow conditions in our 'Goretex' sleeping bags, waking up to the early morning sunrise, which was quite magnificent. Later we made our way down to a much needed cooked breakfast and mugs of tea.

The Ring of Steall is another amazing ridge with numerous airy sections. I and other climbers had to cross a wire bridge, high above the turbulent river, which comprised only three wires, one for your feet and two for your hands; it was like a swaying tightrope. As a precaution we had to undo our rucsacks around our middles in case we fell. Part of the Ridge was above the 300-foot Steall waterfall which provided unbelievable views. It was amazing coming down in the dark after eight hours using our head torches to pick our way through the snow.

I've enjoyed climbing all the ridges in Wales, with Crib Goch on Snowdon being a particular favourite of mine. The sensation of scrambling along knife-edge ridges with their high and exposed sections, together with the breath-taking scenery is magical, especially when combined with snow and icy conditions.

One time I was on Tryfan and Bristly Ridge, again during wintertime, and on the way down I caught my foot on a crack in a rock and broke my leg. The rescue service was called out by my friends, and members of my team carried me down on a stretcher to the ambulance which was waiting for me in the valley to take me to Bangor Hospital. So, unfortunately, on that occasion I ended coming back home in plaster.

We were once climbing on the Idwal Slabs me when we had the

profound privilege of witnessing a Brocken Spectre, which just stopped us in our tracks. A Brocken Spectre occurs when someone is high on a mountain and there is cloud inversion or other low cloud weather. The sun must be behind the person standing on the mountain and the shadow image is then projected onto the cloud in the same way that an eclipse occurs. When this happens it is almost as if a spectre or shadowy figure appears within glowing rings. These rings are what is called a 'glory', caused by the refraction of the projected light and as such are concentric rings of refracted light surrounding the image on the cloud. Accordingly, the ghostly figure is produced as a result of the shadow of the climber being projected forward through the mist.

Sometimes Spectres appear to be huge, which is probably caused by the presence of the 'glory' and the mist obscuring more familiar reference points with which to judge its size. Apparently the Spectre takes its name from the 'Brocken', the highest mountain in the Harzgebirge of Northern Germany. Although only about 1000 metres high, the Harz region is very susceptible to periods of low cloud and mist, and this seems to have given rise to a lot of legends about the Brocken being the abode of witches and legends similar to those surrounding Pendle Hill in Lancashire. No doubt the appearance of Brocken Spectre' helped to confirm these mystical legends in early German folk stories.

Heinrich Heine, a German romantic contemporary of William Wordsworth, wrote a famous lyrical poem about the mountain and its legends (Der Brocken) and I believe the 'Spectre' was mentioned in this. No doubt this also contributed to the name 'Brocken Spectre', becoming the accepted name for this phenomenon. When I saw one for the first time it was such a marvellous sight, so breathtaking. I'd never seen anything like it before and it felt very spiritual, very ethereal.

One weekend I helped the Snowdonia Rescue Team, which was a very rewarding experience for me, especially when I went out with them on a mock rescue. We had to find a 'victim' lost in the snow, and then, once we had found him, radio for the helicopters to come.

I was lucky enough to accompany the 'victim' in the helicopter and observe how everything proceeded from there. They were all wonderful people, giving up their time voluntarily to help others. We also had first-hand experience of the lifeboats and their use, which again provided us with invaluable insight into the rescue service and its efficiency.

Another time in my life when the adrenalin was well and truly pumping, was when I went on a Land Rover course in Wales. I learnt so much in such a short period of time, including driving up steep hills then reversing back down them, as well as driving through mud and rivers. It was exhilarating and gave me so much confidence, especially having to contour around a hillside, convinced that I was going to tip over at any moment. The instructors assure you about everything all the time, and make you believe in yourself and have faith in your vehicle. I had a fantastic sense of achievement at the end of the day but was exhausted with all the concentrating. Roy met me afterwards and took me for a much needed coffee as a pick me up.

My true love now is the Lake District. It is so beautiful, and spending the day walking the ridges is so rewarding. There is nothing better. We spend many weeks up there walking in all

On the shore of Buttermere looking towards Fleetwith Pike.

weathers. Each season tells a different story. I have walked and climbed in all parts of the Lake District, from ice climbing in the gullies of Wetherlam to trekking over Crinkle Crags in Great Langdale. The latter is quite rough underfoot and along the traverse of the five summits but that is all part of the adventure together with the numerous rocky boulders. Leading on from this you arrive at the 'Bad Step', a rocky ten-foot-high block which is near vertical and provides an exciting obstacle to overcome. The Bowfell Climbers' Traverse is another great joy, a narrow track below the cliffs, and then there is the awe-inspiring Bowfell Buttress, where we climbed in earlier days and which would uncover lots of hidden secrets as you progressed.

I've always enjoyed Pillar from Wasdale. We were once out enjoying the horseshoe when a friend of mine decided that we should scramble up the soaring cliffs of Pillar Rock. What a wonderful sight greeted us and all thoughts left my mind in the excitement of it all. Of course we then had to come down the same way, which made for quite a hairy descent downwards!

Sharpe Edge on Blencathra has always called to me as well. The sharp-edged crags fall away in near vertical fashion and there is one spot where a slab slopes so steeply that you have to shuffle across

Helm Crag from Graasmere Lake.

41

in a sitting position. The summit rewards you with beautiful views as well as a large cross made of quartz, which greets you on ascending. How on earth it was ever placed there is anyone's guess but it is quite beautiful to behold.

I've spent many days on Great Gable and climbed it so many different ways, with its scree running down to the valley below. Then there's the famous Napes Needle on Great Gable, which we once climbed during a thunderstorm terrifying but invigorating, especially as we abseiled down it as the lightning flashed all around us. The Napes ridge comprises of rock which is very exposed. We arrived back following the climb in a state of near collapse but having loved every minute of it.

Nowadays, more often than not, we tend to walk the Fairfield Horseshoe, which we are very fond of now, together with Steel Fell and the Silver Howe ridges. When climbing the Fairfield Horseshoe, we stay in a cottage quite close to it in Grasmere. As long as we have our prerequisite bag of sandwiches and a flask we are more than happy, and totally in our element.

Before the accident, and having climbed every mountain in the Lake District, I decided I wanted to have a change of direction and to enjoy the fun of scrambling, especially the Ghyll scrambles, which were so appealing in terms of their excitement.

Fleetwith Pike, Warnscale Bottom, Great Gable, Haystacks, High Crag

Pillar Rock in particular was a great scrambling route as it comprised some awkward steps and some highly exposed positions followed by a seriously steep descent via the Slab and Notch. We would usually end up soaking wet at the end of the day, with me having fallen in water more times than I can remember but that was all part of the fun.

Sourmilk Gill in particular is in a brilliant situation and of course you can finish your climb by visiting the summit of Great Gable and then maybe onto Needle Gully and the Sphinx Ridge. Crinkle Gill, in the Langdales, is an interesting way to climb higher when traversing Crinkle Crags and in turn get spectacular views and fine rock scenery. We always seemed to get drenched on this scramble, which only added to the fun.

Easy Terrace on Dow Crag was another favourite of mine with Dow Crag being the real magnet in terms of attracting climbers to the Coniston area. As part of the climb there are some steep and exposed rock moves, which make this a serious situation to be in, though my favourite of all was Pinnacle Ridge on St Sunday Crag. This is a very exposed crest to traverse, causing the adrenalin to really surge around your body, heightened also by the particular weather conditions of the day. We would also quite frequently visit the 'edges, e.g. Sharpe Edge and Halls Fell Ridge on Blencathra, and, of course, the very popular Striding Edge on Helvellyn, which would

When at Loughrigg, on a summer evening, 'listen to the silence' and the peace all around you. Loughrigg is a most peaceful corner within the Lakes.

never fail to provide a rewarding day out.

We now spend most of our holidays in Grasmere. We love the gentle beauty of the Lakes, especially Loughrigg Tarn with the backdrop of Loughrigg Fell and its dramatic views of the Langdale Pikes in the evening light and the idyllic scenes while walking in Little Langdale. Equally pleasurable are the walks alongside the tumbling Sour Milk Ghyll en route to Easdale Tarn.

The fells around Grasmere are just so lovely. There are wonderful secret places on Loughrigg Fell with delightful grainy paths, which offer lots of pleasant surprises. There is so much of interest on this fell for everyone to enjoy; the walks are so rewarding with wonderful views over Rydal and Grasmere. Roy and I never tire of traversing the rocky slopes of delightful Silver How with its juniper shrubs, gritty ridges and rocky, narrow ledges over Megs Gill, which tower over the waterfalls. It is steep initially but well worth a visit.

We never leave Grasmere without spending time walking over Helm Crag, a splendid climb among the juniper-clad rocks. The summit

At the edge of Rydal Water looking back towards Nab Cottage and Nab Scar.

has so much character and is so unusual, in such an interesting way with its steep rough crags. The ridge takes in the summits of both Gibson Knott and the rocky crest of Calf Crag. We also make our way over the delightful Steel Fell. I personally feel that everybody who stays in Grasmere should find time to do this wonderful excursion with its flanks falling to the secluded valley of Greenburn, it makes for such a happy day's walking.

We love to wander on through to 'The Secret Garden'. This is my interpretation of a beautiful, large, walled-garden estate, it is so mysterious and magical and has some small ponds and lots of wildlife. If you are lucky an inquisitive deer might drop by or you sometimes see them peeping at you from behind the trees. Herons and badgers are always visible and on occasion you can see woodpeckers. The beauty of the wild flowers there never changes and being there and experiencing nature at its best is such a wonderful way to end a perfect day. Many people don't know of this place, I like to keep it a secret, it is so enchanting. It is almost as if you can hear the birds and animals talking to one another. I first found this place with my eldest granddaughter, Alex, and needless to say it holds a special place in my heart; hence our decision to give it the name 'The Secret Garden'.

Langdale Pikes, across Loughrigg Tarn.

For us, several weeks a year are spent at Tongue Ghyll, an idyllic place looking out onto the slopes of Helm Crag. It is so lovely there as you encounter the soothing sound of the waterfalls of the Ghyll together with the frequent visits of the woodpecker, which we enjoy watching for hours from the lounge window of the cottage where we stay. Two ducks also visit us whenever we are there. They sit and wait at the back door so patiently at breakfast and at teatime for little titbits. Then satisfied, they waddle off to ride down the waterfall.

Weekends are spent at the cosy 'Silver Lea' on Easdale Road, a central point for our favourite walks; if you are awake at about 3a.m. you may be lucky enough to see the badgers toddling across the path under the lamp post, which is quite lovely to watch, and well worth being awake for at that time. The woods nearby are full of badgers, evident by the large badger holes they leave behind. Quite frequently deer visit the garden. jumping over the fence to enjoy the flower tops. Often in the middle of breakfast we will leave the table to chase off the deer which have been busy helping themselves to tulips for breakfast. Our weekend would then never be complete without fish and chips at the 'Jumble Room', our favourite restaurant in Grasmere, which we feel is well earned after a time walking in the fells.

On the way down Red Bank with a view of Grasmere,
Helm Crag and Sea Sandal

Chapter 6

Work and Pleasure

With the children having left home I decided to look for work again. This was a little bit daunting having spent so much time at home. Saying that, I was fortunate to find a series of jobs, first working as a supply secretary at Lowton County Primary School for a year in 1981, followed by five years at Golborne Saint Thomas Primary School from 1982 to 1987, and then finally Lowton West Primary School from 1987 to 2007.

Looking across Loughrigg Tarn

I definitely felt as if I had fallen into a niche, as I was using a lot of the skills I had acquired during my secretarial course, which had lain dormant for a while, but were now all coming back to me; I was fortunate to be working with great staff members. Most importantly I loved having the children around me with their amusing ways and their endearing qualities - well mostly!

I used to take the children to Hinning House, an Outdoor Education Centre in the Duddon Valley in the Lake District, where we would climb, go caving, mountain biking, canoe and go orienteering. It was a fantastic experience both for the carers and the children, and so rewarding for us to see them having such a carefree time. They seemed to flourish from the experience and used to go home imbued with a sense of positivity and enthusiasm and a more open, responsive approach to life.

Thirty years later, children, whom I had accompanied on the trips used to come and see me and reminisce about the good times they had had. Certain experiences and adventures would stick in their minds including the midnight walks through the forests and

Birks Bridge – River Duddon

swimming in the river - experiences they probably would never have had with their own parents; but that's what it was all about, allowing them the freedom to be themselves away from the confines of everyday life.

Another wonderful memory I have, is of me and the children running down to the river in the mornings, with towels around our necks, to have a wash. It definitely beat washing in the bathroom! I remember in particular, one young lad of about ten, complaining in his broad Lancashire accent about the water being too cold, and me with a perfectly straight face replying that if he felt under the rock nearest to his hand, he would find a button underneath it. If pressed, it would heat up the stream. The look on the little boy's face when he did as he was told and innocently remarked that the water was definitely much warmer now was priceless! What innocent fun we had!

Of course this all seemed like an adventure to them and they loved it. Sometimes we would sleep in the local fells near the centre, all in a circle, with goodies to eat and hot chocolate to drink. Other times we would sleep all night around a fire or walk the fells and come down with our tents, put them up and cook tea. Whatever we did the great outdoors seemed to fill all our hearts with tremendous joy and happiness.

Camping in particular was always great fun with the familiar smell from the surrounding fields of dung, the need to get the kettle boiled to make that essential cuppa first thing in the morning as well as the incessant creepy crawlies at night and the pitter patter of rain on your tent. There was one particular time when the rain was absolutely pouring down and I was bursting for the loo. But it was pitch black outside and I was in the middle of a field and had absolutely no intention of going outside. I gave it a moment's thought and then spotted the nearest thing to hand, which just happened to be the pan we had cooked the beans in that evening. Without any hesitation, I did what I needed to do, slung the pee out of the tent door, closed the zip quickly and swiftly went back to sleep. Needless to say the beans were well flavoured next morning and nobody was any the wiser.

In my experience I've found that it always pays to camp near the edge of a wood for numerous reasons. You can usually find a good spot to use as a toilet, without prying eyes, camouflaged by thick branches of spruce scattered in every direction; also the soft moss carpeting the forest floor would also be a bonus offering kindling and sticks. The downside, however, would be the midges which would follow you everywhere, so we would always get the fire going very quickly. Another occasional downside of camping was the very large slugs that I would from time to time find in my sleeping bag together with newly formed molehills underneath our tents. On one occasion I remember having to move to another spot as it was just like a minefield outside. The compensation for all of this was watching the magnificent, flickering lights of the campfire in the evening and the dying embers at the end of the night.

My favourite activity with the children was the 'Lone Walk', where the children went off in teams of six without an adult, following a written, illustrated map. I would creep alongside, well hidden, sometimes with a tree branch in front of me. Other times I'd be crawling in the bracken or sitting up in a tree keeping an eye on them and enjoying listening to some of their funny conversations. Towards the end of the walk, I would discreetly run to the minibus and stand where they could see me. Their little faces were a picture with relief, happiness and pride written all over them. I would have hot chocolate and chocolate bars ready for them. They were so happy, they would chat and laugh throughout the drive back to the Centre. Needless to say they slept well that night. It was so rewarding to see children enjoying themselves in such a way in such an enchanting valley.

Sometimes we would also take the older children to Hinning House which was great fun for us all. The teenagers found the great outdoors 'real cool' and very different to their everyday life at home, which to them seemed boring in comparison. Besides the camping and walking in the outdoors, we would take them caving in Yorkshire, squeezing through a tunnel eight inches wide called the 'cheese press'. Needless to say they all found it very scary and daunting; some needed a little 'persuasion' to get through but after coming out at the other end, later on that day, they were thrilled they had done it and assured us that they wouldn't have missed it for the world.

One lovely girl was blind and insisted that she rock-climb up a steep face. I went alongside her, both of us roped up, giving her a little advice, encouragement and confidence. She did brilliantly and by feeling for hand and footholds managed to get to the top. We both ended up shedding tears of happiness once we made it. She showed remarkable courage in what she had done and for me experiences like that made everything so worthwhile.

Each morning while staying at Hinning House at about 6.30a.m. we would go for a run to Cockley Beck and back which was about two miles. On returning we would go for a wash in the river before having a wonderful cooked breakfast - happy days!

Each morning when the breakfast was being cooked, a little face would appear through the kitchen window. It was Fuchsia, a sheep, who obviously got quite hungry when the bacon smells wafted across his field - can you blame him! Then when nothing came through the window he would slide inside to salvage any leftovers. The school children gained so much from their week there, such as team work, communication skills, character building which I am sure helped them so much when they left school, and entered the big wide world to forge out careers for themselves.

Sometimes when the children had the week at Hinning House we would take them to the other Outdoor Centre, Low Bank Ground at Coniston. We would take two minibuses over the Wrynose Pass to canoe on Coniston Water. This was always great fun, as first they would be issued with wetsuits, which would always set them off into fits of laughter while putting them on. More often than not, just as they had got the wetsuit all zipped up they would want the toilet! So, off would come the wetsuit followed by more peels of laughter. Once they had grabbed a life jacket each, we would go off down the hill to the water where they were given canoes and clear and strict instructions.

Sometimes we would all go off for the day to Peel Island, which is in the middle of the lake and quite a long way away. But they were mostly all capable of doing this. Once there, we would have lunch and swim and play in the water, mostly pretending it was a smuggler's island, just to add to the drama and fun of it all. Of course, then we had to head back to the Centre, with everyone, needless to say, tired but exhilarated. All the children would be nodding off on the way back to Hinning House in the minibus but at least for a while it was quiet!

As well as the outdoor pursuits with the children, I also used to enjoy caving in Yorkshire with other adults, where we would come across fast floods and high waters. First we would abseil through a hole in the hillside and use rope ladders to traverse the interior. It was nerve-wracking, as occasionally we crawled through narrow tunnels for six hours or more. Such hard physical activity, as you can imagine, was exhausting, but also gave me such a sense of elation and achievement once we had made it to the other side.

So many funny moments have sprung to mind while writing this book, I remember one time when I had been canoeing on Coniston Water with other adults and I desperately needed the loo. So I left my canoe on the bank and ran into the forest on the advice of one of my colleagues. He had assured me that it was a secluded spot where I would have the necessary privacy. So there I was answering the call of nature when totally out of the blue a team of runners came directly across my path. Well, I was like a stunned rabbit caught in the headlights but worse because I was mortified with embarrassment with nowhere to turn. In a blind panic I put both legs in one knicker leg, and somehow hobbled somewhat ungracefully back to the group. Worse still I had to drive the minibus back in that state. Needless to say the guys at the Centre howled with laughter when I told them what had gone on. For me these things just seemed par for the course.

Chapter 7

Tragedy

It was to the outdoors I turned in 1988 and in particular the solace of the Lake District Fells, when Roy and I were faced with the most devastating and traumatic period of our lives. The loss of our beautiful youngest daughter, Lesley, in a car accident. She was only eighteen at the time and had been travelling in her red MG Midget from her friend's house one night - having decided not to stay over as she had originally planned - along Holcroft Lane from Rixton towards Culcheth near Warrington.

When she went missing it was as if someone was physically twisting my heart, an awful all consuming pain. In an instant everything around us changed from the norm into something hellish, an overwhelming blackness, where everybody close to Lesley was immediately filled with a sense of total fear and desperation. Life as it was, was immediately put on hold never to properly resume again as it turned out, well not as it had before.

As the police investigation began and an almost surreal set of events took over, including appeals by ourselves on the local News for sightings and information on our missing daughter.

It was a devastatingly traumatic time in our lives. I remember my other children being there and trying to offer each other comfort as best we could, despite being numb with shock and overcome with feelings of despair. After fifteen days Lesley was finally found. She had come off the road in her car. The verdict stated that it was an accident as there was no alcohol in her blood, which tied in with the fact that she had a very clean-living approach to life.

Roy and I were bereft, our worst nightmare had come true. I felt an array of searing emotions over the following months and years, ranging from anger that such a wonderful, vibrant person had been taken from us so young, to deep, deep feelings of hurt that caused me to ache physically and caused longing for her voice and her presence again.

That year, 1988, was a terrible year for us. My own mother, understandably, was totally devastated when Lesley died and would six months later succumb to pneumonia and herself pass away that year. My father had died thirteen years previously at the age of sixty-one from a brain tumour, which took him suddenly after spending a happy week at our caravan on Anglesey.

I have never got over losing Lesley. People say that time heals but it doesn't and I think we have all been left badly scarred by this single event. I do think though that she has been around me since; I have felt her presence. Without doubt, I feel she helped me get through the terrible accident that I would later have in the Cairngorms. I think she was guiding me, protecting me and it gives me such a profound sense of comfort to think that she was with me, and is with me, and we still have that connection to this day.

I think, as I have mentioned already, the deep loss we experienced and this caused us to increasingly look to the great outdoors for solace and to replenish ourselves in some way. Roy and I loved holidaying in the Alps, Switzerland being a particular favourite with its glittering lakes hemmed in by beautiful snow-capped mountains and wonderful fairytale features. Wild and snowy places have always held a great fascination for me. It was with this in mind that we travelled to Grindelwald under the awe-inspiring Eiger, which was to provide an amazing experience for us.

Different nationalities were camping there when we arrived and the atmosphere was tremendous. Lots of climbers were sitting there, waiting patiently for nightfall and for just the right weather conditions to climb the notorious North face of the Eiger. Obviously, less than perfect conditions could prove fatal. We camped there too and sometimes, at night, you could hear chamois, a type of deer, creeping and sniffing about being inquisitive. Camping in Lauterbrunnen was equally lovely and provided us with wonderful memories of the lovely Trimmel Valley. How lovely it was to witness nature at its finest and to wake up each morning to the sound of cowbells rather than the usual shrill alarm clock!

We also travelled to the famous railway station at Kleine Scheidegg where the train passes through mountain tunnels and past glaciers before proceeding to the highest station in Europe, the Jungfraujoch at 11,333 feet. This railway, on which work commenced in 1912, ended up being the most expensive ever to be built in the world.

You can watch the climbers on the notorious Eigerwand while you are ascending the mountain by train; once at the top you can walk to the climbers' hut situated on the Eiger crevasses, where the snowscape surrounding you is breathtaking. We did this trip a few times, in varying weather conditions, and I remember one time when a storm suddenly came in, which proved to be a particularly hair-raising time for us but immensely enjoyable nonetheless.

We stayed in a hotel in Wengen in 1989, a charming village, which you have to access by mountain train as it is traffic free, which was a special holiday organised for our twenty-fifth wedding anniversary. It lived up to all our expectations and proved to be a fantastic Break walking daily and climbing vertically up rock faces using ladders and traversing ledges hardly wide enough to allow you to walk upright. There were wires attached to the rocks for us to hold onto and to steady ourselves, which helped, but it was still pretty precarious especially as we had to use the wires to swing round to other rocks and ledges. This definitely got the adrenalin pumping and required nerves of steel, especially as we had to descend the same ladders that we had previously used to ascend the mountain. To say it was exhilarating is an understatement!

Another notable holiday was a stay on the borders of Switzerland and France, at Chamonix, which was a beautiful spot. We used to walk parts of the Mont Blanc circuit, which was truly inspirational in terms of its beauty, providing mesmerising views.

One day we decided to go in one of the lifts up Mount Blanc, so we waited quietly in the queue in soaring temperatures. After a while, I grew impatient with all the waiting and the hustle and bustle of tourists around me and persuaded Roy to give it a miss and to go and have a drink instead followed by a a walk later on. A short while later, having a drink outside a Pub, we heard a terrific bang followed by a large flash. A storm had suddenly come in from nowhere and proved to be a real stinker. We were so relieved to have given the mountain lift a miss.

On arriving back at our hotel that evening we learnt that the lift had been caught up in the storm, high up, and left hanging there for hours. Understandably everyone inside was panic-stricken and traumatised by the whole proceedings. Some of our friends were on this lift and they didn't get back to the hotel until morning. What a frightening experience it must have been for all those inside, thinking the lift could possibly fall at any moment It had been so fortuitous for us that we had avoided the same fate.

Nowadays we go to Austria, and have been doing so for numerous years. Obergurgl is my favourite place with wonderful scenery and wild and rocky parts. The vibrant colours of the Alpine rose and gentians just heighten the experience for us, providing such natural beauty. Together with the vistas, you can hear the shrill whistle of the marmots perched on rocks warning their companions of imminent danger, as well as the chamois roaming the rocks and the lovely 'Haflinger' horses in the valley.

Memories of other holidays remain firmly at the forefront of my mind, particularly a stay in Elmau one year. This was a happy time for us but going up high with a guide to the Elmau Top with only wires to hold onto, passing over sheer drops, was truly terrifying. On reaching the top the guide got out some Schnapps and asked us to drink down a dram in one go. We obliged of course! Not to do so would have appeared rude.

We were then told in broken English, (which only seemed to add to the drama of the situation) that we would be going down the mountain the quick way, whatever that was, and naturally we just looked at one another, wide-eyed. It turned out that the quick way was scree running all the way down, no stopping! Well, without doubt, it was the speediest way to descend the mountain but certainly not the kindest in terms of our poor bodies. We didn't know what had hit us and we were absolutely exhausted by the time we reached the bottom; once there, we couldn't stop laughing, the whole experience having been such a thrill.

All the mountains have lovely huts to stop off at for much needed respite, which usually included beer, lovely thick goulash soup and fried potatoes, which always proved to be a real treat. The food in Austria is wonderful, especially the 'Grosti' (fried potato with pieces of bacon topped with an egg). Once we ordered a mushroom omelette each at lunchtime thinking it would be nice and light but not taking into account the Austrian's generous portions We were amazed when they were brought to our table, still sizzling in their skillets, and found to be huge, comprising six eggs per omelette, per person! And that wasn't all, it was then accompanied by fried potatoes. Needless to say we put some real hard work in, climbing for the rest of the week, to burn off all those excess calories

Chapter 8

Ben Macdui

I found planning our trip to Braemar in Scotland very exciting. I had always wanted to climb the mountain ranges in that area of Scotland and this represented a fantastic opportunity. The idea all came about when two of the friends I was with at Hinning House Outdoor Centre asked if I would like to join them that coming February half-term, camping and climbing the mountains around Braemar. I thought this was a great idea and readily agreed.

First of all I had to make sure I had all the necessary equipment including ice axes and crampons. This was particularly necessary as the climbing was planned for the month of February when the weather can be extremely cold with the ever present threat of ice and snow. I also ensured that we carried adequate provisions and this included the baking of fruitcake and ginger biscuits for both me and my climbing companions. Tents and camping equipment and our bikes were also needed as we would be staying at a campsite in Braemar the night before our planned climb with a view to then ascending Ben Macdui, Derry Cairngorm and Lochnagar mountains.

To familiarise myself with the area, I read numerous books on the mountain range and did my research. Here is an extract from a guide for mountain walkers called '*The High Mountains of Britain and Ireland*' by Irvine Butterfield describing the range:

Ben Macdui 4296 ft/ 1309 m
Ben Macdui, its five tops and its satellite peaks, Carn a' Mhaim, Beinn Mheadhoin and Derry Cairngorm are so inconveniently scattered that even the most zealous (climber) might find it tiresome to sweep them all into one day. The latter two plus six tops are therefore grouped into Walk 4 leaving a manageable but still awkward expedition based on Ben Macdui.

The construction of the road to Coire Cas detracts from the rigours of the Cairngorms, and on a walk to Macdui may well do the walker a disservice by denying him the benefit of a gradual attunement to his surroundings. Ben Macdui (also known as Beinn Mhic Dhuibh) can be reached from Cairn Gorm by a long level walk across the plateau. Several crude paths in the turf lead to the head of the Feith Buidhe and the stony rise to Macdui's north top. But this approach is unsatisfactory for Britain's second highest peak, and for a fuller appreciation of its magnificence it should be approached from the glens of the Dee or from the Lairig Ghru.

The upper hill on Ben Macdui is a vast boulderfield, whose highest point is crowned by an Orinance Survey pillar and an indicator, erected by the Cairngorm Club in 1925. On a clear day the views are extensive and embrace the whole of northern Scotland.

Duly informed about the terrain and well prepared in terms of provisions, we spent our first night at Braemar camping, and the following morning, the day of the climb, we checked the weather forecast for the day, which was quite good.

Suitably reassured we prepared a packed lunch and made sure we had extra clothing in our rucksacks such as gloves, hats and balaclavas. I had an extra '*Buffalo*' jacket rolled up and most importantly a survival bag together with a compass, map, head torch, whistle, ice axe and crampons.

Leaving the campsite early that morning we planned our route and decided to cycle in for about three miles through the native pine forest filled with sheltering herds of deer. It was a very treacherous bike ride in the ice and snow, especially with all my gear attached to my back, and I seem to recall falling off three or four times. The views were stunning though and we were feeling very buoyed up. Deciding to leave our bikes at a designated spot with a view to collecting them on the way back, we set off for the mountains, aiming first for Derry Cairngorm.

The going was steady for a few hours but then the weather seemed to deteriorate quite quickly making the climb more and more hazardous. Despite this we carried on climbing even though we were finding it harder and harder to find our footings and soon found ourselves slipping and falling more and more frequently. Somewhere along the way we must have branched off, joining the path to Ben Macdui. By now the weather was turning pretty nasty, but I persevered, even though disturbingly for me, somewhere along the way I had lost my two friends. By this time walking was getting really tough and fatigue was setting in. It was a hard struggle. A blizzard was approaching and it looked increasingly as if a complete white-out was inevitable.

I particularly remember at that time the massive cornices hanging over the edge like huge jaws, making me shudder every time I glanced at them. I was getting really anxious by now and was desperate to get off the plateau. This should have been the most exhilarating plateau walk the Cairngorms had to offer but it was becoming fraught with danger. The terrain underfoot was incredibly icy and there was a high snowbase. Trapped by a blizzard, as I now was, I had to envisage all possible scenarios and weigh up the options. I knew the Ben Macdui edges in a white-out were treacherous. With this ever present in my mind, and in the dense mist, tears began to flow. I cried. Then it happened. Without warning, the snow gave way on the corniced ridge. I never even saw the crack and I plummeted through a hole into the snowy void hundreds of feet below. All the time I was tumbling, strangely without fear at this point, I felt only a sense of numbness.

Scotland's second highest mountain is a featureless dome and for me at that time there was no trace of the top. Panic was setting in. I was all alone. Snow and cloud merged to form a blank whiteness, while spindrift flowed continually down the slope and threatened to push me off. I needed to get back to Braemar. I started shivering. Frantically I dug into the cold wet snow, I knew I had to get shelter, if I were to survive the night.

I was sixteen hours on the slope of Ben Macdui, in minus 40ºC temperatures, not daring to move for fear of falling. The unrelenting wind was gusting the snow into my freezing face and forcing itself through the tiniest of openings of my clothing. I was shivering uncontrollably. I knew after this length of time that I was in serious trouble and close to exhaustion. I couldn't bring myself to look down me, knowing there were probably more steep snow slopes below. I was alarmed at my behaviour, my shouting, which proved futile as my words were continually whipped away by the wind.

The morning came, without me having slept and it was still a white-out. I was stiff and frozen and I decided to chance climbing down the slope. I had lost my ice axe. It was to be a slow and careful descent using my fingertips to feel my way down. But it was a chance I had to take, either that, or just lie there and most certainly die. It had been an endless night being there all alone, and climbing out took hours. The slope seemed to become steeper and as the cold and exhaustion increasingly set in, I wanted to cry, out of a mixture of panic and fear. I eventually landed on a flat plateau, where I used my warming routine of slapping, banging and rubbing, to keep the driving cold away as best I could.

It was a wild and unforgiving place up on that mountain and I was so cold and so exhausted that after a while I began hallucinating, not that I recognised it as such at first. I saw people, different individuals, none of whom I knew and I even spoke to them. But they remained resolutely silent. Inanimate objects also appeared in front of me - houses, bikes cars, roads and then simply vanished and in their place I was shocked to be confronted with just another snowdrift.

I knew I was in desperate trouble and close to death. Hypothermia was setting in. This happens when the body's core begins to freeze as a result of exposure to extreme weather conditions. More often than not this condition happens to young people as they are more vulnerable than adults in terms of their mental and physical reserves. Because hypothermia is a condition where there is a progressive fall in the body's core temperature, if you don't get help quickly, it can lead to unconsciousness, heart failure and even death, especially when combined with exhaustion and can kill quickly. This is why emergency gear while mountaineering is so essential.

I ate snow constantly to try to keep myself hydrated and struggled on through snowdrift after snowdrift, the winds constantly driving the snow higher than myself.

Suddenly I stopped dead in my tracks and questioned myself as to what had just manifested itself directly in front of me. It appeared to be a railway crossing barrier which had dropped from nowhere straight ahead. I reached out to touch it but as I did so it disappeared, leaving nothing but a huge cavernous hole in its place, thousands of feet deep, which menacingly opened up in front of me. It sent a chill down my spine, I was on another cornice.

I turned to my right and another barrier dropped. Again I tried to touch it but again it disappeared, and another hole appeared. Terrifyingly for me I was still on a cornice. I walked back the other way. Whatever had caused this apparition to appear, it was warning me of imminent peril, and without doubt it saved my life. I felt, as a result, that someone was with me, a strong, indefinable presence.

Although this feeling provided me with some comfort, the harsh reality was that I seemed to be fading. I knew the situation was extremely serious for me and that I was very close to death. I kept thinking back over many years and the people I had known during my life, especially my family whom I loved so dearly. I had so much to live for and I was determined to fight all the way.

The cold was insufferable, more penetrating and biting than I had ever experienced before. It was even painful to breathe and take control of my muscles. Fear kept coming over me in waves, though by this point there were no tears - the snow I had eaten obviously not having provided enough for my body's requirements - just this damned shivering with me hunched over hands between my thighs desperate for warmth.

Then, out of the blue, a strange thing occurred. I suddenly found myself being dragged, at speed, horizontally through a dark tunnel, towards a bright light at the end, then a sensation of floating and detachment. I seemed to be walking through a beautiful, other-worldly land where everything was bathed in a pale blue and white light even the trees and bridges, a bit like a scene taken from the famous Japanese 'Willow Pattern' china, and where everything was silent and calm.

I progressed towards the light and felt at peace, happy, oddly detached and free from the cold and the misery. It was one of the most serene and contented feelings I had ever experienced. I felt at the same time that I wasn't alone, almost as if I was being accompanied by a friend - again that overriding sense of a presence. How long this lasted I will never know, but after observing my body on the mountain hundreds of feet below for a while, I soon found myself back in the freezing weather conditions again but somehow imbued with a fresh sense of strength and courage to go on.

I persevered, and battled on, even though my reserves were now nearly on empty and my cagoule was frozen solid around me. I felt as if I must rest, recharge my batteries, especially as darkness was approaching once more. But I knew that I must not go to sleep because if I did, I knew that I would not wake up. My throat was dry and sore and I was, at this point, partially blind. What had caused this frightening condition I later found out, was total exhaustion. This snow blindness that I experienced was extremely painful and felt as if my eyes were full of sand, making blinking excruciating together with exposure to light.

With what was left of my strength, I built a snow shelter with my frozen fingertips, to enable me to bed down for the night, which seemed to take an age. I knew that without it, I wouldn't survive the night. The windblown snow and deeper drifts provided excellent building material and, once complete, I crawled into the shelter and huddled in my polythene survival bag, desperate for sleep. I managed to avoid doing so by singing silly songs and repeating my warming routine.

I was colder than I could ever have imagined possible and shivering uncontrollably, though the air in the shelter was quickly heated by my body's warmth. I was tremendously weak and lay in the silent darkness, craving drink, and cramming more and more snow into my mouth, which didn't seem to help at all and only served to make my mouth more sore.

I lay huddled in the snow shelter until dawn with only a small hole in the shelter to use as an escape if need be, over which I had placed my rucsac as a makeshift door. Above me I saw my survival bag floating away in tiny pieces - another hallucination - as after my rescue, the bag was found folded up in one piece in my rucksack.

The next morning overriding thoughts of getting off the mountain crowded my mind as I knew my chances of survival were now slim. I crawled out of the shelter. Nothing had changed, it was still a white out with blustery snow. I no longer knew what to do, then to my total amazement a large bright 'V-shaped' light suddenly appeared from nowhere, then in an instant it had gone. I struggled to put my compass on the ghostly light but, despite this, it had given me enough of a clue and I knew instinctively that it was showing me the way off the mountain.

Experts and those who believe in such matters say it was a 'guardian angel' and I tend to agree with this view. Whatever it was, it gave me the strength and the sense of direction to take action. I soon found myself sliding and tumbling down an icy waterfall of melted snow before landing uninjured in a valley. I heard running water under the ice and I crawled along the snowy surface.

Then I saw people and a dog. I questioned myself as to whether they were in fact real following my earlier experiences and fought back tears of relief as I realised that they were. I was on the brink of collapse but overwhelmed with a profound sense of relief.

I will never forget the warmth and kindness that the Rescue Team showed me on that day and the dog licking my face to resuscitate me. Despite having ended up with frostbite in my fingers and feet - which is a freezing of the flesh on parts of the body, usually the face, hands and feet. At least I had survived the experience and kept all my digits intact. In fact the greyish white appearance and feeling of numbness through prolonged exposure to wet, cold conditions in time disappeared, though this was a long and painful period of recovery. Fortunately, I wasn't left with any permanent tissue damage. I am only too aware it could have been far, far worse, avoided largely by the prompt action of the hospital staff on my arrival. Fortunately for me too, the blindness quickly disappeared and my eyesight returned to normal as usually happens within a few days. My throat took a lot longer to heal but that too recovered in time.

Apparently while I was missing, the media were out in full force, wanting to know all about me and why I was in the predicament I was in. Camera crews had decamped not only to Scotland but also outside my home in Lowton and were interviewing everyone they could, whenever they could, to get an angle on the story and taking lots of photographs.

As well as talking to neighbours, they were even at the school where I worked speaking to friends, parents and colleagues. A television crew even interviewed the Deputy Head at his home, the upshot of which later became a bit of a standing joke between us as he said in all sincerity about me, "Well, she doesn't feel the cold too much. She never wears much in school!"

Not only was it of local interest but also it was on the national news and later on, the story would even gain international interest. I was part of the national news coverage worldwide for about three nights. My sister-in-law was in America at the time and couldn't believe it when I suddenly appeared on the big screens in the Centre, close to where she had been skiing that day. At that time, she didn't even know I was missing, so it was quite a shock. Another friend was in Tenerife and out walking when she saw me on the front of a newspaper, which understandably for her seemed somewhat surreal.

Most of the coverage was extremely positive and supportive.

In one newspaper report it described how "*Survival experts praised the 5 ft 2 in school secretary, who took up mountaineering only five years ago, for her courage, her preparation and her common sense. Facing blizzards that reduced visibility to a few feet, she stuck to her survival training and dug into soft peat to shelter from the murderous wind.*" Captain Alan Sylvester, Head of the RAF Kinloss Rescue Team that found her at 9.20 a.m. yesterday after she had spent her second night on top of 3,788 ft Derry Cairngorm, said, "*She had one hell of a will to live*".

The report later went on to say, "*Experts said Mrs Greaves owed her life to proper training in survival techniques which ensured she went properly equipped. She wore thick gloves and socks and heavy duty mountain boots. She is also understood to have been wearing thermal underwear and a man-made winter fleece sweater, designed to retain heat. Her outer shell clothing was made of 'Goretex', which also 'breathes', allowing condensation to escape.*"

Support too from the staff and pupils at Lowton West Primary School in Greater Manchester where I was a school secretary was overwhelming. Teachers and children alike frequently visited my house to bring cards and presents. Here's a selection of the ones I received:

Dear Jackie,

God must have been working overtime! I've never heard of so many people praying for one person! You'd be amazed how many people couldn't sleep Monday night and spent the time drinking coffee etc. I bet it shows up on the National Grid.
Love Gillian and Ian.

Thank God you made it. You scared the hell out of us. We're thinking of roping you to the coach on the 27th. Next time you want to spend some time alone, let me know and I'll lock you in the bathroom! I've never known so many people to burst into tears on hearing two words. Are you sure it's only blood in your veins and not 50% Guiness?
Love Pat.

Here are some sent to me by the children, including spelling mistakes!:

To Mrs Greaves,

My Mum could not get to sleep. I hope you get better soon. We care about you. I sore you on the news and the newspaper, it wos on the Big Brefes as well. I wont you to come to school.
Love Siobhann.

To Mrs Greaves,

You can climb a mountain and count Dinner money too. Your a very special person so get well soon.
Lots of love Suzanne Wilson.

Dear Mrs Greaves,

I hope you are better soon. I can't what for you to come bake to school. I am very sad about you. I am very very very glad that you are still alive - you are my best secretary.
From Stacey-Anne Houghton
Class 7.

Dear Mrs Greaves
I found your story fascinating. You were very brave. I was worried when you were missing but very very glad when you were found. Your a STAR!!!!!
lots of love Kelly, Class 9
P.S My Mum and my big sister were worried the most.

The most poignant and moving of all the letters though has to be the following one, sent by a complete stranger, with the one intention of extending a warm hand of kindness:

Dear Mrs Greaves,

We were overjoyed to learn of your survival from the accident on the mountain.

Having heard of your plight through the media on Sunday, I remembered you in prayer and the next morning my prayer partners and I came together to pray for those in need.

We prayed that the Lord would meet your needs - protect you and help you to find a snow hole - and direct you to safety. Another Christian friend brought me the Daily Mail giving your address, your account of the incident, which I have read with interest and indeed amazement at your courage and strength, against the elements.

What a blessing you have been saved to continue onwards and upwards.

I often think of John Wesley's words: 'I was saved to serve' when he was rescued from his burning house, while still a small child. None of us know when we may need help but, we are thankful for all the carers and their dogs or any other aids used to save lives.

I too share your love of mountains, although I hasten to add I'm no climber, just a walker given strength, sight and hearing to share the beauty of Gods creations.

I used to live in E. Africa, where on a clear day, I could see Mount Kenya from my breakfast room window - hundreds of miles away! A truly majestic sight and as awe inspiring as Mt Kilimanjaro rising straight from the plains in Tanzania to 19,000 ft.

Looking too, more like a giant Christmas pudding with cream running down its sides!

The power of prayer is really tremendous. We have seen many remarkable answers to prayers, perhaps not always what we had expected, but He always answers because He knows what is best for us.

I think it's all very wonderful that the prayers offered on your behalf from Christians all over this country, and maybe beyond these realms, have truly and wonderfully been answered - in that you are fully restored to full health after your frightful ordeal

God bless you and all your dear relatives and friends.

Yours most sincerely. With Christian love,
Kate Elizabeth Bell. SRN

However, as is the norm in life, there were also one or two detractors as the following article taken from the Daily Mail, 16th February, 1994 indicates;

'The Cost:

74 volunteers, one helicopter and a bill for £150,000.

The rescue operation was one of the biggest of recent times and is expected to cost more than £150,000.

The cost will be borne by the RAF and the Mountain Rescue Associations involved.
Most expensive was the Sea King helicopter from RAF Lossiemouth - around 40 hours at more than £2,000 an hour. More than £70,000 was also spent on equipment and other essentials for the 74 rescue workers at £25 per man hour.

The searchers, mostly volunteers from the RAF, the police and the public, combed a massive area of the Eastern Cairngorms. A

*majority were civilians, some self-employed, who gave up two days'
pay.*

*The 22 strong combined Braemar/Grampian Mountain Rescue Team
started the search at 9p.m. on Sunday. Eight police officers and 14
volunteers split into two groups and a helicopter from RAF
Lossiemouth was put on stand-by.*

*Appalling weather conditions forced one team to abandon the search
and dig in on the mountain top. The second team searched through
the night until 6 a.m.*

Teams from RAF Kinloss, RAF Leuchars and 16 volunteers from
the Aberdeen Mountain Rescue Team joined the search on Monday.
Now 74 strong, the team which included one dog, searched from 8
a.m. until 4.30 p.m, resuming at 6.30 a.m. yesterday with a further
eight dogs from the Search and Rescue Dog Association.

Nearly three hours later Mrs Greaves was found. But rescue leaders
stressed the cost would be borne either by the RAF or by the
individual Mountain Rescue Associations. Team leader Graeme
Gibb said they estimated that £25 per man hour was spent on food,
equipment and other essentials. *"We also have fuel charges, the
running of the rescue centre and other costs to find,"* but added. *"The
burden will be spread. Each civilian mountain rescue team absorbs
its own costs. The RAF treats an operation like this as a training
exercise and also absorbs all its own costs."* He said the only people
who would be out of pocket were the volunteer rescuers.

Lord Hunt however, leader of the British expedition to Everest in
1953, also lent his voice to the critics, and was quoted as saying the
following:

*"To fall through a cornice... is a risk that should not be taken in
conditions of high wind and poor visibility. Indeed, it was
irresponsible folly to have ventured at all on that high and exposed
plateau in such weather"*, he thundered in the correspondence
columns of the Independent.

"What is more deplorable, however, is that the rescue of this lady, albeit thanks to her personal resolve and good equipment, should have cost the taxpayer a large sum... In the Alps such rescues have to be paid for by the victims or their dependants."

When interviewed by The Times newspaper on 25th February, 1994 and asked in response to such criticism whether I agreed that mountaineers ought to insure themselves to pay the cost of rescue, I was quoted as saying, *"No, that would take all the joy out of it"*.

The article went onto say how I had indeed been told that the rescue helicopter would have been flying whether I was there or not.

As for the rescue team, the paper reported me as saying *'their payment is to pick somebody up alive'*, which I can't recall saying, adding the quote *'I do lots of charity things and send money to the rescue regularly'*.

The article concluded that I would certainly send some money to the rescue team if I got any, but also added that I seemed uncertain that the tabloid newspapers would come up with anything, let alone the fabulous sum of £20,000 bandied around. As it turned out I did receive this amount, which I duly donated to rescue teams in the area to purchase a rescue dog and a vehicle.

While this was all happening there was little that Roy, David and Sharon could do but sit tight. It must have been an awful ordeal for them. They have later said to me though, that despite the unknown, they all had an inner feeling that the chances of me surviving might be higher than outsiders might think.

They knew I was tenacious and a fighter and would be determined to find a way to survive. Because of this sheer bloody-mindedness they knew there was a chance of me coming home safely and because of this they still had hope and they clung onto that.

The following was reported in the Daily Express on Wednesday, 16 February 1994:

We never gave up hoping.

Jacqueline's family last night spoke of their joy at her rescue.

"I never gave up hope" said her husband Roy. "But today was the day of reckoning. If she had not been discovered, then even I would have feared the worst. She has plenty of experience in the mountains and is very fit. All along I thought that would carry her through"

The ordeal was a repeat of the agony the family went through five years ago. Their 18 year old daughter was missing for a fortnight before her body was found in her sports car. It had crashed off a road not far from their home. But while it lay undiscovered, it led to fears that she had been abducted and possibly murdered. After the latest scare, Jacqueline's family will be trying to persuade her to give up the dangers of Scotland's peaks and concentrate on the more gentle Lake District.

Mr Greaves, 52, a Building Agent, who prefers rambling in warmer weather and lower slopes, confessed that he was unlikely to keep his wife off the hills. "What can I do? Tie her up? Take away her car?" he said.

But daughter, Sharon, 26, believes that her mother's ordeal will keep her on safer ground.

'I think we will put her off this. From now on it will be gentle walks in the lakes.'

Sharon revealed that her mother had survived for an afternoon in a mountain-top blizzard once before by digging a snow hole. She had also once broken her leg while climbing in Wales and had to be rescued. "She is truly amazing" said Sharon. "Mountaineering is her life. It has been a terrible two days."

Arriving back in the helicopter at Raigmore Hospital at Inverness was quite something. There were hundreds of people there waiting for me to arrive. I couldn't understand at first why they were there, but then realised they were there out of kindness and I found it deeply touching.

But the media was a different story. They were crowding the hospital trying to get the facts and even went as far as to be in my ward, which was hardly conducive to my well-being and the well-being of the other patients.

I obviously wasn't well and needed treatment. The doctors put me in a warm bath, raising my core body temperature slowly, after which I was wrapped in warm towels. I eventually started to come round and warm up, except for my fingers, which were rigid and numb due to the frostbite and would take a time to heal.

Mentally I was struggling. The papers wanted my story and wanted to take me somewhere quiet away from the hospital but the doctor said that I wasn't well enough and that I would put my life at risk if I left. I stayed at the hospital and allowed journalists to sit by my bedside to record what had happened. They paid me for this, but I was frightened of keeping the money, feeling I hadn't earned it. I accepted the cheque, but bought a lovely 'Search and Rescue' dog for a rescue team. They called it 'Guinness' in acknowledgement of my love of the drink.

Over the years I am proud to say he has saved quite a number of lives. Also I helped to buy an ambulance for another rescue team, whose vehicle had just been written off in an accident. The rest went to children's charities. This gave me a wonderful feeling that I was able to help others.

Because of all the media interest Raigmore Hospital, Inverness released me secretly once I was feeling well enough to leave. I was taken through a small back door at the rear of the hospital in the middle of the night with my hood tightly pulled up. Looking back now it seems amusing, farcical even, but at the time I felt like a rabbit caught in the headlights dazed, disorientated and vastly unprepared for what lay ahead.

But there was nothing that could prepare me for the media onslaught, and for my emotional response to all of this, and not least to what had just occurred on Ben Macdui. To say it was an unsettling time for me and all those around me is a huge understatement.

For a start when the media found out that I was now at home, it was as if the immediate area was under siege. The Avenue, where I lived, was crowded with cars, journalists and cameras. It was so congested that the bins couldn't be emptied that day as the wagons couldn't get anywhere near. Inside the house the phone was constantly ringing – not the best environment to make a speedy recovery I might add. Outside it was 'bedlam' with repeated knocking at the door and ringing of the bell.

Fortunately as the days passed the intensity of interest waned, a sense of normality returned, at least to the outside world if not to my own. The immediate family tended to me and helped me to recover remarkably quickly. But the mental scars, the psychological aftermath which I was keeping secret to myself for fear of people thinking me mad, were all too vivid and would take a much longer period to heal.

Chapter 9

The Aftermath

After the accident, life changed significantly for me. I was taking extra care with things I did, especially when I was on the mountain tops. Even now when I'm on the ridges and the mist or the snowstorms come in, I get a sort of panic in me which I have to quickly overcome. Before, I would have a go at anything and never seemed to see the danger in it. In other words I lived quite dangerously and never seemed to have any fear. Indeed after the accident my family and friends said I was a changed person - less selfish. I did lose confidence and that was the downside. Conversely I gained so much more awareness of, and respect for my own safety

Calf Close Bay, Derwentwater, drawn on a perfect, still sunny day in May.

and the importance of recognising the preciousness of life, thereby living life to the full everyday but without taking unnecessary risks.

I know now that I am an extremely lucky person to have survived such an experience and very much felt that I had been given a second chance. I count my blessings every day and very much live life to the full, almost as if on a mission. When I can, I try to respond to the needs of others more and help the less fortunate as much as possible. This takes the form of leading people on mountain walks and sharing the great pleasure of the solitude of the mountains. I also organise a fellwalking club, which has become very popular with all ages from about thirty to seventy-four years of age. There is a lot of fun and friendship involved and sometimes a meal at the 'Horse and Farrier' in the North Lakes to end a great mountain day. I also try to help by visiting the elderly, raising money for charity and giving talks to young people in schools, which I find extremely rewarding.

It has only been quite recently that I have found out that this kind of experience where an individual feels the presence of an invisible force is quite common, and is such a widespread phenomenon that it even has a name: the 'Third Man'. This name is thought to derive from the biblical story in which a resurrected Christ appears to two of his disciples on the road to Emmaus and walks alongside them. Apparently it has been experienced by mountaineers, polar explorers, divers, prisoners of war, solo sailors, astronauts and even '9/11' survivors. All have escaped traumatic events only to tell similar stories of having experienced the presence of a companion and helper. The presence offered a sense of protection, relief, guidance and hope, leaving the person convinced he or she was not alone.

The most famous encounter and one later recorded in verse by T S Eliot in his poem 'The Waste Land' (who is the third who walks always beside you?) - is that of Ernest Shackleton.

Towards the end of the Imperial Trans-Antarctic Expedition of 1914-16 at the point where Shackleton and his two surviving crew faced almost certain death, he reported an unseen presence joining them.

Their ship, the '*Endurance*', was ice-bound and Shackleton and two others set off on foot to cross the treacherous ranges and glaciers of South Georgia to reach a whaling station.

The march took 36 hours and some years later Shackleton confided to a journalist, "it seemed to me that we were four, not three." Although Shackleton said nothing to his companions at the time, the others later admitted they had also experienced, "a sense that there was 'another' person with us." Surely all three could not have imagined the same thing? Then, in the decades following Shackleton's mystical experiences on South Georgia, there was a flurry of Third Man reports. They occurred around the world under extreme, but also very different conditions. Some, like Shackleton's, appeared to be corroborated by more than one witness.

So why the sudden proliferation of Third Man stories? One theory is that the nature of exploration itself altered at around this time. Instead of large ships carrying scores of men, or vast columns of soldiers. explorers began to travel solo or in small groups. Henry Stoker, a submarine commander and distant relative of Dracula creator Bram Stoker, wrote about how he and two others escaped from a Turkish prisoner of war camp and attempted to cross 350 miles of rugged terrain to reach the coast with neither maps nor compass and only meagre rations of raisins and cocoa powder. Hungry, thirsty, footsore and dispirited, Stoker became convinced a fourth man had joined them and found his presence deeply comforting. When later he discussed it with his colleagues, he realised they too had experienced the same thing.

The phenomenon continues to this day. Peter Hillary, son of Edmund experienced a strange presence during an expedition to the South Pole in November 1998, retracing Scott's final Antarctic journey. In this case, Hillary knew the 'entity', which appeared to him and guided him; it was his late mother, who had died in a car crash more than twenty years earlier. "It was like she'd come out there to keep me company," he said. In a similar vein, diver Stephanie Schwabe escaped certain death when she heard the voice of her late husband and diving partner, Rob Palmer.

Diving in an underwater cave off South Bahama Island in August 1997, Stephanie lost the guideline - which led back to the entrance - and began to panic. Convinced she was going to die and still desperately missing her husband, she gave up on life. Then at the height of her desperation and sadness, she recalls, "I suddenly felt flushed and it seemed like my field of vision had become brighter." She believed the 'presence' to be her dead husband and heard him mentally communicating with her, calming her and instilling a belief that she would survive. Calmed by the presence, Stephanie discovered renewed resolve. This time she slowly and methodically scanned the cave and just as she saw the flash of a white line, the 'presence' left her. Swimming immediately to the line, she followed it to the surface and emerged unscathed.

For others, the 'Third Man' is not nearly as personal or easy to identify. But it is no less efficient. For example on the morning of 11th September, 2001 Ron di Francesco was at his desk at 'Euro Brokers', a financial trading firm on the 84th floor of the South Tower of The World Trade Centre. When the first plane hit the North Tower at 8.46 a.m., in what was to become the biggest ever terrorist atrocity on US soil, di Francesco and his colleagues were initially told that there was no threat to their building and to remain at their desks.

Fortunately he had already started to vacate the building when the second plane slammed into the South tower. Because he had left the office di Francesco was hurled against the wall and showered with debris but survived the devastating impact. The trading floor he had just left no longer existed.

He made his way to an emergency stairwell and following the advice of others gathered there, decided to ascend and wait for emergency services to rescue them from the roof. By the time he reached the 91st floor, the intensifying smoke caused him to panic and he changed course, groping his way down the staircase. On the 79th floor, he fell to the concrete floor with a dozen others, gasping for air. They were prevented from descending further by a collapsed wall and even through the fug of smoke, the panic was evident in their eyes. Some were crying, some slipped into unconsciousness. And then something remarkable happened.

Di Francesco heard a voice - not one of the group - address him by his first name. It told him to get up. The voice was insistent but encouraging, and was accompanied by a vivid sense of a physical presence. "Somebody lifted me up. I was led to the stairs. I don't think somebody grabbed my hand, but I was definitely led."

The benevolent helper guided di Francesco down the stairs, insisting he walk through fires, which he did covering his face, before continuing to make his way down. Almost an hour after the second plane hit, di Francesco reached the ground but as he headed for an exit the building began to collapse. He heard 'an ungodly roar', saw a fireball and fell unconscious, later waking up in hospital.

Ron di Francesco was the last person out of the South Tower. A lot of people made split second decisions that day, which determined whether they lived or died. What is different about di Francesco is that at a critical moment he received help from a seemingly external source. A deeply religious man, di Francesco is convinced he experienced divine intervention.

Looking back I recognise now that surviving those days on the mountain was an amazing achievement, and just being alive and reunited with my family and friends was obviously a huge cause for celebration and thanks. Despite this however, I struggled to come to terms with what had happened on the mountain and especially the 'out of body' episode that I had experienced. I had never even heard of this before, let alone experienced it; I felt, out of a fear of being misunderstood or thought crazy, that I couldn't tell anybody and so kept all these thoughts and feelings to myself, which really didn't help matters.

Physically, I seemed to recover quite quickly with the frostbite healing after a few months of pain. However, this feeling of detachment that I had had since the accident continued in the following months, together, most disturbingly of all, with visions , at night time of our daughter whom we had tragically lost a few years earlier.

All this caused me to struggle emotionally to get well. Night-time in particular was awful with these visions appearing in front of me and a sense of falling which I couldn't control. At these times it was like reliving the event and fear would engulf me. I kept questioning myself as to what I had witnessed and the nature of it. What had been the light watching over me? Why did the 'V-shaped' light appear? My mind was whirring and working overtime. I increasingly went off to the Lake District to escape these awful sensations and find refuge. I needed to be alone and I walked the hills for miles and miles, until gradually and slowly I started to feel better.

I later found out that extensive research has been undertaken into what are called *'near death experiences'* (NDE'S) and that the first major publication dealing with such experiences was Dr Raymond Moody's *'Life After Life'* (1975), in which he came up with a model encompassing all the elements of typical 'NDEs'.

During his research Moody interviewed more than one thousand people, who claimed to have undergone an 'NDE'. From his research he identified ten features that he said defined the near-death experience. Although very few people claimed to have experienced all ten of these, most reported five or six. Here are the common features:

an awareness of being dead (though for some this only occurred later in the NDE),

an out of body experience where there was no pain only peace,

the feeling of travelling through a tunnel, or passing through doors or up a staircase

meeting people of light, usually deceased relatives or friends,

viewing idyllic countryside, scenery or cities,

meeting a 'being of light', which some identify as God or Jesus a review of one's life,

rising or floating into another realm, where the physical body cannot enter but human consciousness can,

reluctance to return,

the sense of entering another dimension where there are no constraints in terms of time.

Since the publication of '*Life After Life*', many more books dealing with 'NDE's have been published and as a result, it could be said that this has led individuals to be influenced by something they have read. Yet the range and variety of people who have experienced 'NDEs' seems to dispel this theory, as despite their different backgrounds and cultures, there are so many consistencies in their reports.

I have also subsequently found out that the 'out of body experience' (OBE) seems to be a common feature of many 'NDE' experiences. Light is of great significance also, a brilliant, golden white, which is so vibrant it is otherworldly but at the same time is not painful to your eyes. There is this common consensus that it seems sourceless and omnipotent and that the closer you get to it the more strongly you can feel what can only be described as pure love, in which you are totally immersed. All time seems to stand still and everything feels right as if this is the perfect place to be. In the midst of what the author Ronald Russell calls 'this timeless perfection', however individuals - much as I did - become aware that there is a definite 'presence' there with you. It is not a person, but a 'being of light' that connects with your own consciousness. For me this was just a 'presence', for others it imparts information or messages.

For those, who experience it, the meeting with the 'being of light' is usually the most memorable feature of the 'NDE'. In terms of the light, it seems to make no difference where the experience takes place, whether following a road accident, in the home or out in the open, or after a climbing accident as in my case. In every major religion light is of enormous significance, a uniting symbol between faiths and so it seems to be with 'NDEs'.

In Moody's first book he used the expression '*the experience affects his life profoundly*' of someone who has had an 'NDE'. Further research has tended to conclude that a 'NDE' has a profound effect on those who experience it. A fascination with these after-effects led Kenneth Ring in his book '*Lessons from the Light*' to state that in all the cases he has studied the individuals '*though still diverse in their personalities, tended to share a common psychological profile afterwards. In short, most of them appeared not only to be transformed by their experience, but transformed in much the same way.*"

The elements of this profile are as follows:

enhanced appreciation of everyday life

greater feeling of self-worth and self-acceptance

increased concern for others and wanting to help others reverence for nature, the planet and animal and plant life

a rejection of materialism and unnecessary acquisition

an anti-competitive attitude

a more spiritual and open-minded approach to life

a quest for more knowledge

a new found sense that life is meaningful and full of purpose for everyone

no fear of death

a belief that some form of existence follows on after death

a certainty that another spiritual entity and place exists.

Chapter 10

Return to Normality

Following on from the accident various people and organisations showed a great deal of kindness to me. The 'Guinness' Company, for example, sent a can a day, for the next three years to my house. The wagon would roll up at my house with its delivery and cause quite a stir with the neighbours in a nice kind of way of course! After that they would send any cans I requested and I ended up carrying forty-eight of them on my back in a rucsac up Great Gable in the Lake District, straight up the waterfall of Sour Milk Ghyll and onto the summit. It was quite a weight but well worth it because I would sell the cans en route for a donation - one kind person actually gave me a ten- pound note for one can. I managed to raise a few hundred pounds each time, which I then sent to the 'Search and Rescue Dogs Association' (SARDA). The dogs there are fantastic, saving countless lives annually, and of course 'Guinness', the rescue dog I had bought, was a member along with the rescue team, who had brought me off the mountain.

Naturally I have been interested in the progress of 'Guinness' over the years and have kept in touch with his owner. The following is taken from a letter he sent me quite recently, providing background to his training as a search dog in the early years and the work he had been involved in since.

I had been a dog handler for eight years when I got Guinness as a puppy from a rescue centre. He was very nervous and timid, particularly around men. Guinness was a Labrador, Collie cross. He ate like a Labrador but had the brains of a collie.

When I started to train him he was about five months old and I had to work on building up his trust in me. He was already showing real interest in his squeaky toy though, which was a good sign, as these toys play a large part in training a search dog- they are their reward when they find someone. In order to train them you get someone (what we call a 'body') to go and hide with the toy, then the handler sends the dog to find the 'body', who when found, plays with the dog and the toy. In turn the handler then praises the dog. Basically we brainwash the dog into thinking that anybody lost has a squeaky toy in their pocket.

It took two years to train Guinness to search dog standard, although he was on the call out list after one year as a novice dog, so he could learn searching skills. In training we normally give a dog and handler an area which comprises an hour long search but during the real thing you can be searching all day or night. The handler breaks the searches down to about an hour with a stop in order for the dog to rest and be given a treat and for us to have a cup of tea; this interval ensures that the dog's interest is kept at a high level.

During Guinness' working life as a search dog, we did well over one hundred call outs. We had only one find during that period and unfortunately the person was dead when we found them. The rest of the time, during the searches we played a large part in helping to find the missing person, whether it was a missing hillwalker, missing child or OAP. We were saving both the police and the mountain rescue team's time as a dog, in good conditions, can do the work of up to twenty people.

Guinness was ten when we retired from SARDA. We were both sad to stop but my hips and knees had had enough and dictated that I couldn't really carry on. This meant no more telephone calls at two or three in the morning to go on a search, followed possibly by a drive for three hours before you even got there. As a handler in 'SARDA', you can be called out anywhere in Scotland 24/7 every day of the year - and we call it volunteering! 'SARDA' still continues

*to train dogs and handlers to this day and anybody interested in
finding out more about the work of this organisation can easily do
so by using our website address*
http://www.sarda.org/.

People continued to be kind to me well after the accident. I was also
sent lots of jam, peanut butter and chocolate spread from a very
considerate jam firm, most of which went to the Outdoor Centres in
the Lake District, where I worked voluntarily with the children
doing outdoor pursuits. This went down a treat, of course, especially
the chocolate spread, and kept them going for months.

I continued to receive mail and what I found most touching was the
nearly four hundred cards and letters that I received from all kinds
of people and from all over the world in the aftermath of the
accident. They were all so lovely and considerate, sending their best
wishes and prayers. It gave me an uplifting feeling that the world
really was full of lovely, caring and kind-hearted people, who
wished others well. This feeling was increased by the flowers that
were sent by people, who didn't even know me.

As well as newspaper coverage following the accident, I did a few
television programmes, which were filmed in Scotland Making these
with the lovely film crew was really fun to do. This positivity all
helped me to feel so much better. I also did more and more walking
and climbing in the Lakes - taking the schoolchildren to the outdoor
centres as much as possible. We also went climbing, biking and
extreme caving in France and even cycled parts of the Tour de
France.

My accident continued to attract interest mainly from magazines
now. The following, for example, is an article from the TV Times,
1994.

*She was lost in the mountains. It was minus 37° F, pitch black and
snowing. Then Jackie Greaves saw a dazzling light - did it save her
life?*

As she lay frozen on the steep, icy mountainside with gale force winds and temperatures of -37° F, Jackie Greaves was certain she was going to die.

An experienced walker, she had never before felt so cold or so alone. But then a miraculous series of unexplained visions seemed to guide her safely off the mountain.

As the 'Strange But True' programme reveals this week, there had been no indication of the nightmare to come. It was a cold, clear day in February last year when Jackie, 53, a married mum-of-two, set off with friends to walk through the Cairngorm Mountains in Scotland.

"Gale force winds came from nowhere", says the school secretary from Lowton, Greater Manchester. "There was a white-out and as we turned back, I lost my footing and fell through a huge hole in the snow."

When Jackie eventually came to a halt, still on the steep, snow-covered mountainside, she saw her first vision. "A white light, like a torch beam, was shining at me all night," she says. "I thought it was another climber but no one came, yet the light stayed all night."

For seventeen hours Jackie lay on the ice, too terrified to move. She had food in her survival kit and 'drank' by melting snow in her mouth. But when dawn broke, she knew she had to get off the mountain or risk dying of hypothermia. So she started inching downwards on her stomach and eventually reached a flat plateau piled high with snow drifts.

It was then that Jackie had two visions which almost certainly saved her life. "Suddenly a railway level crossing barrier came down in front of me but when I leaned out to touch it, it disappeared. Underneath it was a big hole about forty feet deep. I'd have fallen into it, if the barrier hadn't appeared. I changed direction but after another few yards a similar barrier dropped down. It, too, vanished when I tried to touch it, and I saw another hole there. Then the strangest thing happened. I felt like I was being dragged away by a strong wind. Suddenly I was in another land. There were blue skies, blue flowers, even the grass was blue. It was beautiful. I was away from all the fear, cold and misery. I felt at peace."

Jackie believes she was so close to death that she visited 'the other side'. The next thing she remembers is being back in the snow but with renewed strength to carry on. Amazingly, she endured another night in sub-zero temperatures before her final vision guided her to safety.

"The next morning, I saw another light and set my compass to that point", she says. "I lost my footing again and started falling down the mountainside. I tumbled for ages before landing at the bottom. Then I could see men with dogs and I thought 'Thank God". Her forty-two hour ordeal was over. She later discovered that her friends had alerted the mountain rescue team but everyone had given up hope of finding her alive because of the terrible weather conditions. She was flown by helicopter to hospital, where doctors were amazed to discover that her only problem was frostbitten fingers.

Looking back, Jackie believes another force was involved in her battle for survival. "It was as if someone was watching over me and they decided my time wasn't up yet. It's still there, because I'm not scared of going into the mountains again. I didn't really believe in the supernatural before", says Jackie today. "but maybe you have to experience it before you can believe in it."

But the biggest legacy from the incident was the need to get out there and help people as much as possible, especially with respect to walking on the fells. Subsequently I have organised a Fellwalking club, which has proved to be very popular and successful.

We go into the hills, mainly in the Lake District, and lead people on lovely mountain walks. It gives everyone a lot of pleasure and relief from the stresses and strains of everyday life, as well as providing much needed fun and friendship.

The Duddon Valley is one of the special places we visit. It is a most beautiful valley, one of the lesser known ones in the Lake District. It is magical with its woods and pastures between the shapely fells of Stickle Pike, Caw and Harter Fell. The river Duddon takes an interesting journey of about seventeen miles along this friendly dale. It passes waterfalls and lovely Seathwaite Church and the only pub in the dale, the 'Newfield Inn'. passes nooks and dells, cottages and farmhouses and, of course, flows alongside Hinning House, where our schoolchildren used to have their morning wash and play happily for hours.

I must admit I have had a few falls along here in my time and have been thrown in the river by the children in fun many times also. I have so many happy memories of this charming valley which will be with me forever.

Undoubtedly climbing the hills gives you a great sense of being alive, there amidst the most breathtaking lake and woodland scenery. I have now climbed every mountain in the Lake District and enjoy them each and every time. Each different season and the differing weather conditions all combine to provide unique vistas and a

Looking onto Rydal Water and Loughrigg Fell from the old road to
White Moss Common and Grasmere

unique type of beauty. Sometimes something extra special also happens, totally unexpectedly, such as the time quite recently, when we were out walking and some wild ponies came over to share our picnic, a truly magical moment.

Walking and gardening are my main passions now. Growing your own vegetables to then pick and eat, right through the seasons, is a constant source of delight for me and gives me such a profound sense of achievement and satisfaction. Needless to say the health benefits are obvious and I believe that if everyone grew just a few vegetables we would be a much healthier nation. The best time for me though is when the grandchildren come round and ask what soup they'll be having that day from the produce I have just gathered up from my garden. It is such a delight to know they are having wholesome food and that we are all taking part in the whole gardening process together.

I also love attending my local 'FX' Gym and taking part in a couple of hours of step aerobics each evening. It gives me such a great sense of well-being and keeps me fit. The girls are all really friendly and we usually enjoy a good chat before we start the class. Penny, our instructor, is great with us and really gets into the swing of things. I come home exhausted but having had a great time. I have made some really close friends there too.

I now have six beautiful granddaughters, Alex the eldest, spends a lot of her time looking after her horse, Sonic, and visits most days to see us and enjoy a bowl of home-made soup. Charlotte calls in each day after school to enjoy some toast and a cup of tea while telling us about her day. Skye. Gracie, CoCo and Honey live a distance away in Leighton Buzzard so we don't get to see them as often as we would like. I miss them very much and am very fortunate to have these six wonderful granddaughters, whom I love dearly.

I know how fortunate I am and count my blessings every day. I am grateful though for the joyous times I have spent mountaineering and can very much agree with the view of Geoffrey Winthrop Young who said:

"Mountain climbing is an adventure: an adventure open before our eyes and more or less accessible. There can be no adventure without uncertainty of its result, and in good adventure, there is also an element of risk, even of danger to life. In climbing mountains, danger is a constant element, not remote as in other sport. It is always with us behind the veil of pleasant circumstances, and it can be upon us before we are aware. The mountaineer, therefore, has to not only know and observe the rules, which govern the good playing of all sport; he has to keep another set of values constantly in mind, values which involve the larger issues of life and death. To lose a game may be beneficial and is always educative; to be beaten on a mountain may incur the loss of life or our own peace of mind."

from 'Mountain Craft' by Geoffrey Winthorp Young. (1920).

Because of the precarious nature of the more extreme climbs and my experience on Ben MacDui, I have learned the importance of compromise. Climbing is still in my blood but now I am happy not to set the bar too high. In this way I am fulfilled. In the words of Frank Smythe:

"When I climb a hill it seems to me that I do not merely exercise my muscles, breathe pure invigorating air and pursue a technical interest. I am happy. The rocks, snow and ice that I tread may be defined as chemical substances, the height I gain be estimated as a measurement, yet these things together produce indescribable effects on mind and spirit. I count myself fortunate to have trodden the heights of the Alps and Himalayas, to have sat with friends by camp-fires, to have tramped the heather of the British hills. And more than this, I am happy in the memories of these things. To climb a mountain is to tread not only the heights of the Earth, it is to adventure to the very boundaries of Heaven."

from 'Mountain Vision' by Frank Smythe.(1941).

*'Every year that passeth, the true mountaineer crosses
another contour line on his journey through life.
Now and again he comes across a line which is
shaded a little darker than the rest.
At such times we should pause,
reflect a little and gird up our loins for the
struggle that lies ahead.'*

From 'The outlying Fells of Lakeland' by A. Wainwright (1974)

FROM BOTH SIDES NOW

Bows and flows of angel hair,
And ice-cream castles in the air,
And feather canyons everywhere:
I've looked at clouds that way.

But now they only block the sun;
They rain and snow on everyone.
So many things I would have done,
But clouds got in my way.

I've looked at clouds from both sides now,
From up and down, and still somehow
It's cloud illusions I recall,
I really don't know clouds at all.

Moons and Junes and ferris wheels,
The dizzy dancing way you feel,
As every fairy tale comes real:
I've looked at love that way.

But now it's just another show;
You leave 'em laughing when you go.
And if you care don't let them know,
Don't give yourself away.

I've looked at love from both sides now,
From the give and take and still somehow
It's love's illusions I recall,
I really don't know love at all.

Tears and fears and feeling proud
To say 'I love you' right out loud,
Dreams and schemes and circus crowds:
I've looked at life that way

But now old friends are acting strange;
They shake their heads, they say I've changed.
But something's lost, but something's gained
In living every day.

I've looked at life from both sides now,
From win and lose, and still somehow
It's life's illusions I recall,
I really don't know life at all.